Numeracy for Teaching

Derek Haylock is Senior Lecturer in Education at the University of East Anglia Norwich, where he is Co-Director of Primary Initial Teacher Training and responsible for the Mathematics components of the primary programmes. He has worked for 30 years in teacher education, both initial and in-service, but he also has considerable practical experience of teaching in primary classrooms. His work in mathematics education has taken him to Germany, Belgium, Lesotho, Kenya, Brunei and India. He is co-author (with Anne Cockburn) of *Mathematics in the Lower Primary Years* (Paul Chapman Publishing, 1997), co-author (with Doug McDougall) of *Mathematics Every Elementary Teacher Should Know* (Trifolium Books, Toronto, 1999), co-author (with Marcel D'Eon) of *Helping Low Achievers Succeed at Mathematics* (Trifolium Books, Toronto, 1999) and author of *Teaching Mathematics to Low Attainers 8–12* (Paul Chapman Publishing, 1991). His other publications include seven books of Christian drama for young people and a Christmas musical (published by Church House/National Society), and frequent contributions to education journals.

Numeracy for Teaching

Derek Haylock

Paul Chapman Publishing

First published 2001

Paul Chapman Publishing
A SAGE Publications Company
6 Bonhill Street
London EC2A 4PU

SAGE Publications Inc
2455 Teller Road
Thousand Oaks, California 91320

SAGE Publications India Pvt Ltd
32, M-Block Market
Greater Kailash – I
New Delhi 110 048

Library of Congress Control Number 2001132901

A catalogue record for this book is available from the British Library

ISBN 0 7619 7460 1
ISBN 0 7619 7461 X (pbk)

Typeset by Pantek Arts Ltd, Maidstone, Kent, England
Printed in Great Britain by The Alden Press, Oxford

Contents

Read this first

The professional context of teaching

Numeracy for Teaching is a book that, in a way, I wish I did not have to write. Of course, I am in favour of the idea that teachers, in all phases and in all subject areas, should be able to make decisions and judgements based on numerical information with confidence and a reasonable level of accuracy. Indeed, for any group of professionals, this would be a laudable aim, the achievement of which would contribute to all of us having a greater sense of general security as we go about our daily business. I am always pleased to take any opportunity to contribute to raising confidence and reducing the widespread anxiety about working with mathematical ideas that all of us who work in teacher training continue to meet in every new group of trainees. I have worked in mathematics education long enough to understand where these anxieties come from and to realise that they need a serious and sympathetic response.

My misgivings arise from the current professional context of teaching. We now work in a field where those in control of educational policy have an obsession with reducing everything in education to numbers, tables, charts and graphs. There are people out there who actually believe that by improving the statistics you necessarily improve the quality of education. The educational 'newspeak' of today is littered with the language of standards, baseline assessment, target-setting, action plans, performance indicators, value-added data, levels of achievement, average points-scores, thresholds, quartiles and percentiles, Ofsted grades, audits, league tables, and so on. This, we are led to believe, is modernising the profession. Within the Department for Education and Skills (DfES, formerly the Department for Education and Employment) there is a powerful group called the Standards and Effectiveness Unit. Within that is the School Effectiveness Division and within that the Pupil Performance Team. I'm not making this up, honest! The main function of these groups seems to be to gather and disseminate huge quantities of statistical data about pupils and schools, mainly focused on levels of attainment in national tests and public examinations. As a consequence, educational achievement and practice are defined by sets of numbers. Each year this standards unit sends out to schools an 'autumn package' of statistical information. This is intended to enable schools to judge their performance against national standards and against the achievements of other similar schools. 'Similar' schools are determined by the proportions of pupils known to be eligible for free school meals, which is apparently a reliable predictor of the mix of social groups from which the school draws its population. Comparisons with the achievements of these similar schools are key factors in the judgements made by Ofsted inspectors about how well a school is doing. In some cases I have known headteachers to actively seek out the one or two more pupils they need to move them into a different band for free school meals, where the comparisons will be more favourable! This is the kind of daft thing that happens when too much significance is given to numerical indicators in judgements about the quality of teaching and learning.

So, is this the brave new world of teaching? Of course, it isn't. The real world of teaching is still the delight of a teacher interacting with the hearts and minds of young people, the encouragement of seeing genuine learning taking place, and the occasional thrill when a pupil shows enthusiasm, flair and creativity. It continues to be about developing the skills you need to manage a class of 30 uncooperative individuals on a Friday afternoon in a mobile classroom and finding ways of making your material interesting and relevant to their needs and interests. These are the real joys and challenges of teaching.

But the other stuff won't go away. So we just need to make sure that we can handle the mathematics, that we can make sense of the numbers and that we are not being hoodwinked by those who credit the numerical data with unjustified reliability or validity. This book is intended to make a small contribution in this respect. If you have taken the trouble to read my ramblings so far, then you will appreciate why the occasional touch of cynicism will emerge in the material that follows. I find it helps to keep me sane in today's educational climate – and I would recommend a small dose from time to time, particularly when the latest batch of DfES documents arrive at your school.

The QTS numeracy test

One of the consequences of all this is that the DfES has required the Teacher Training Agency (TTA) to introduce a Basic Skills Test in numeracy for all new entrants to the profession. It is no longer possible to achieve Qualified Teacher Status (QTS) without passing this test. The test focuses mainly on interpreting the kinds of statistics that occur in the autumn package, presumably as a way of raising awareness of this annual document within the profession. I suppose it must be a bit galling for the standards unit to keep churning out this stuff, knowing that in most schools it gets no further than a cupboard in the headteacher's office. So, one of the main purposes of my writing this book is to provide teacher-trainees with help in preparation for the QTS numeracy test.

Artificial questions

I have tried as far as possible to set the material of this book in the professional context of teaching. But, of course, I cannot provide the genuine, meaningful context in which you will encounter the need to use the numeracy skills covered in this book, nor the purposefulness in the questions which would help you to make more immediate sense of them. Just as you will find in the QTS numeracy test, many of my questions will be rather artificial. I apologise now for this, because there is plenty of research to indicate that people are much more successful with mathematics when it is purposeful and embedded in a meaningful context. So, although I have tried to draw as much as possible on the professional context of teaching, please realise that I have had to design my examples with the purpose of explaining and discussing a particular skill or concept, rather than to reflect the reality of professional decision-making.

Sources of data: a disclaimer

This book is not intended to be a source of reliable and accurate statistical data about education! As far as possible I have drawn on actual statistics and other data from individual schools, from the DfES, the QCA (Qualifications and Curriculum Authority), and their predecessor, SCAA (Schools Curriculum and Assessment Authority). I have made particular use of the data available on the DfES website. All the data drawn on in this way is therefore available in the public domain. But, occasionally, in order to make the data more accessible for teaching purposes, I have had to adapt it or prune it a little. In some cases, as will be obvious, the source of the data is my own imagination.

I should also apologise to readers in Wales, Scotland and Northern Ireland. I work in England and I have therefore drawn on data related to the context with which I am personally familiar. I have made a definite decision not to include a few token examples from other parts of the United Kingdom to give the impression that the book draws on the full range of educational contexts. I am confident that the material will nevertheless be useful to such readers.

Feedback from trainees

I have trialled the material in this book with my own students and have been encouraged by their responses:

The material is very helpful indeed as preparation for aspects of teaching and for the QTS numeracy test. The appropriateness of the educational setting of the subject matter of each check-up adds to its usefulness.

It is easy to follow and has clear and straightforward explanations. I found the summary of key points helpful as they are a quick reference to reinforce what has just been read. It is bound to be beneficial in preparation for the QTS skills test.

The book is excellent. I think it will present students and others with a valuable resource, not only to help with the QTS test, but also for teaching. I could see myself using it on a dip-in-as-necessary basis.

Many thanks for letting me work through your sample material. I cannot begin to tell you how much more I have learnt! This has definitely made me feel more confident about passing the QTS numeracy skills test!

I have definitely demonstrated to myself from this material that my ability to complete calculations mentally has increased.

I passed the QTS numeracy test last week after working through this material!

Numeracy

The mathematical material in this book focuses especially on weaknesses in numeracy that are often observed in adults in general, and in teacher-trainees in particular.

Many adults rely too much on using calculators or formal written methods to do simple calculations that could be done mentally. So in this book I emphasise especially the development of confidence in using informal and mental methods of calculation. I am also aware that, when they do have to use calculators, many people use them inefficiently. So, help is provided in this respect as well.

Many readers will have gained a mathematical qualification when they were 16 and not have done any formal mathematics for many years since. Understandably, they will have forgotten the meanings of some of the technical vocabulary of mathematics that is not used in everyday life, words such as *median* or *denominator*. So I have taken into account that they will need to brush up on mathematical terminology, as well as revisiting many of the basic processes and skills in which they feel a bit rusty.

Adults are generally weak in handling the concepts of ratio and proportion. Again, many people tend to rely too much on unnecessarily formal procedures for handling problems in this area. So there is a lot of emphasis in this book on expressing proportions in fraction notation and in decimal notation, and on percentages. For example, you should be able to move freely between $\frac{3}{5}$, 0.6 and 60%. This is an important facility when comparing the ratios and proportions that proliferate in the context of teaching.

The biggest concern for those facing the numeracy test is likely to be the interpretation of government statistics, particularly presented in various forms of tables and graphs. By the time you have worked through this book, you should be able to handle with confidence such things as: means and modes, medians and quartiles, inter-quartile ranges, percentiles, box-and-whisker diagrams, pie charts, stacked-column charts, two-way tables, weighted means, cumulative frequency graphs, and even the DfES's favourite – value-added data.

How to use this book

This is not a book to read. It is a book to *work through*. You need pencil and paper to hand at all times, and, when suggested, a calculator.

It consists of 62 check-ups, each focusing on one numeracy skill or concept. Start by trying the check-up question. The answers will be over the page. If you find the check-up question insultingly easy, then give your back a pat and your confidence a boost and go on to something else. Otherwise, work through the discussion and explanation that follows the answers. This is followed by some 'see also' suggestions. These will be other check-ups that might cover some of the prerequisite mathematics needed, or related areas, or extensions of the material being discussed. I then provide a summary of key points, for future reference and to highlight the main things to learn from the check-up. After this there will be one or two further practice questions. You will usually find it very helpful to work through these to reinforce and to assess your own understanding. Answers for these further practice questions are provided at the end of the book. It is important to look at these answers, because often I have included some substantial teaching points here.

This is not a systematic book and the material does not have to be worked through in the order provided. You will probably find it most useful to dip into it from time to time whenever you have a spare half an hour or so. I assume that you will have done most of the mathematics here before. What you need is probably to revisit and practise skills and concepts from your past, to meet them again in the professional context of teaching, and to be provided with a little more enlightenment here and there about what is going on when you are manipulating and interpreting numerical data.

And finally...

In common with my other books, this one will not bear the kite-mark of the Teacher Training Agency for England and Wales. I continue to turn down all invitations to submit material for this scheme, being of the opinion that intelligent readers are quite capable of deciding for themselves whether or not this book is worth buying, without it first having received the approval of a government agency.

Derek Haylock
University of East Anglia, Norwich

Check-Up

1

Mental calculations, changing proportions to percentages

Without using a calculator, rewrite these statements using percentages:

a) A quarter of the pupils in my class have free school meals.

b) Three-quarters of the pupils in my class do not have free school meals.

c) Seven out of eight pupils in primary schools like their teacher.

d) This year our school had to employ a supply teacher 17 days out of 20.

e) Four-fifths of the lessons observed by Ofsted in our school were good or very good.

f) A total of 273 pupils out of 300 achieved at least one GCSE at grade C or above.

Answers to check-up 1

a) 25% of the pupils... b) 75% of the pupils...   c) 87.5% of primary pupils...

d) 85% of the days...   e) 80% of the lessons... f) 91% of the pupils...

Discussion and explanation of check-up 1

Per cent (%) means 'for each hundred'. For example, 27% (27 per cent) means '27 in each hundred', or '27 out of a hundred'. Percentages are useful because they give us a standard way of expressing proportions. This makes it easy to compare different proportions of pupils with free school meals in two schools if they are expressed as percentages (e.g. 37% and 35%). It is not so easy if all you have is the raw data (e.g. 170 out of 459 in one school and 238 out of 680 in the other).

Many simple proportions or fractions can be easily expressed as percentages, using mainly mental calculations. For example, the fraction one-half ($\frac{1}{2}$) might represent the proportion of a set of secondary pupils who own a mobile telephone. Without knowing how many pupils there are in the set, we can still express this proportion as an equivalent percentage. One-half as a proportion means 'one out of every two pupils owns a mobile'. That's equivalent to 'fifty out of a hundred', or 50%. Knowing this we can easily deduce percentage equivalents for some other common fractions. Since a quarter ($\frac{1}{4}$) is 'half of a half', then it must be equivalent to half of 50%, that is 25%. And three-quarters ($\frac{3}{4}$) will be three times this, which is 75%.

Eighths are a bit trickier. One-eighth is 'half of a quarter', so expressed as a percentage it must be 'half of 25%', which gives 12.5%. Knowing this, you can then work out percentage equivalents for $\frac{3}{8}$, $\frac{5}{8}$ and $\frac{7}{8}$. Actually, in example (c) I found it easier to think 'one-eighth of the pupils do not like their teacher', which is 12.5%, and then to subtract this from 100% to find the percentage who do like their teachers. This works because 100% represents the whole set of pupils, that is '100 out of 100'.

In example (d) the '17 out of 20' is easily converted to an equivalent proportion out of a hundred, just by multiplying by 5. This gives '85 out of 100', which is 85%.

In example (e) we can think of $\frac{4}{5}$ as '4 out of 5', which is equivalent to 80 out of 100, or 80%.

In example (f) we simply divide 273 by 3, to deduce that '273 out of 300' is equivalent to '91 out of 100', or 91%.

See also...

Check-up 2: Mental calculations, changing more proportions to percentages

Summary of key ideas

◆　*Per cent* means 'for each hundred' (e.g. 35% means '35 out of 100')

◆　A proportion can be written as a percentage, by working out the equivalent number out of a hundred (e.g. '7 out of 20' is '35 out of 100', which is 35%; '240 out of 300' is '80 out of 100', which is 80%).

◆　The percentage equivalents of many simple proportions (such as $\frac{1}{2}$ = 50%, $\frac{3}{4}$ = 75%, $\frac{4}{5}$ = 80%) should be memorised.

Further practice

Do these without using a calculator.

1.1   Work out the equivalent percentages for the following fractions and then commit them all to memory!

$\frac{1}{10}, \frac{3}{10}, \frac{7}{10}, \frac{9}{10}, \frac{1}{5}, \frac{2}{5}, \frac{3}{5}, \frac{4}{5}, \frac{1}{8}, \frac{3}{8}, \frac{5}{8}, \frac{7}{8}, \frac{1}{20}, \frac{3}{20}, \frac{7}{20}, \frac{9}{20}$

1.2   A pupil scores 21 marks out of 25 in one test and 17 out of 20 in another. Express these marks as equivalent percentages, to decide which mark is the higher proportion of the total marks available.

1.3   In a school of 600 pupils, there are 126 pupils with English as an additional language. In another school the number is 104 out of 400, Compare these proportions by expressing them as percentages.

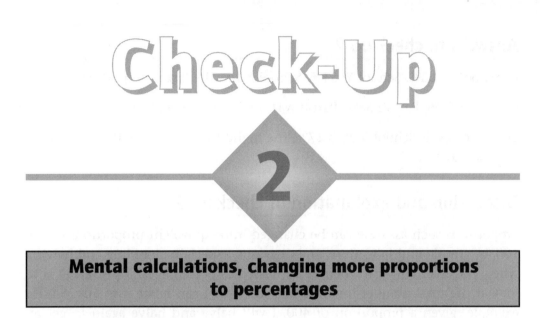

Check-Up

2

Mental calculations, changing more proportions to percentages

Do not use a calculator.

a) School X has 248 pupils out of 400 living within a mile of the school; School Y has 135 out of 250. Which has the larger proportion living within a mile of the school? To answer this, express the proportions as percentages.

b) A pupil scores 22 marks out of 40 for part A of a mathematics test and 39 out of 60 for part B. In terms of percentages, in which part did the pupil score higher marks?

c) Three schools expressed the proportion of pupils on free school meals in different ways.

School A: $\frac{1}{5}$ of the pupils have free school meals.

School B: 17% of pupils have free school meals.

School C: 77 pupils out of 350 have free school meals.

Which school has the lowest and which school has the highest proportion of pupils on free school meals?

Answers to check-up 2

a) School X: 62%. School Y: 54%. School X has the larger proportion.

b) Part A: 55%. Part B: 65%. Part B was the higher percentage mark.

c) The lowest is School B with 17%, the highest is School C with 22%; School A has 20 %.

Discussion and explanation of check-up 2

Proportions such as these can be changed into equivalent proportions out of 100, by simple multiplications and divisions, especially doubling and halving where possible. They can then be expressed as percentages. My strategy is to look at the total number involved and ask how I can relate it to 100. So, for example, given a proportion of 400, I will halve and halve again to get an equivalent proportion of 100. Given a proportion of 250, I will double and double again to get to 1000 and then divide by 10 to get to 100. Below I show how I reasoned for the proportions in these check-up questions. You may well have done these differently, which is fine, of course. I have used an arrow ($\rightarrow$) to mean 'is equivalent to'.

248 out of 400 $\rightarrow$ 124 out of 200 [halving] $\rightarrow$ 62 out of 100 [halving] = 62%

135 out of 250 $\rightarrow$ 270 out of 500 [doubling] $\rightarrow$ 540 out of 1000 [doubling] $\rightarrow$ 54 out of 100 [dividing by 10] = 54%.

22 out of 40 $\rightarrow$ 11 out of 20 [dividing by 2] $\rightarrow$ 55 out of 100 [multiplying by 5] = 55%.

39 out of 60 $\rightarrow$ 13 out of 20 [dividing by 3] $\rightarrow$ 65 out of 100 [multiplying by 5] = 65%

$\frac{1}{5}$ $\rightarrow$ 1 in 5 $\rightarrow$ 2 in 10 [doubling] $\rightarrow$ 20 in 100 [multiplying by 10] = 20%.

77 in 350 $\rightarrow$ 11 in 50 [dividing by 7] $\rightarrow$ 22 in 100 [doubling] = 22%.

Note that in all these questions the relationships between the numbers are such that it is not difficult to manipulate them mentally to obtain proportions out of 100. In the last example it was easy to do this once I spotted that 7 divided exactly in 77 and 350. If, however, the proportion had been, say, 79 out of 350 or 77 out of 352, this would have been far more difficult to handle by purely mental methods and it would make more sense to use a calculator.

See also...

Check-up 18: Using a calculator to express a proportion as a percentage

Check-up 21: Mental calculations, multiplication strategies

Check-up 22: Mental calculations, division strategies

Summary of key ideas

◆   Many proportions can be expressed as percentages by changing them to equivalent proportions out of 100, by simple multiplications and divisions.

◆   Look for ways of using doubling, halving, multiplying by 5 or 10, or using simple divisions to relate the total number involved to 100.

◆   If there is no simple way of changing a proportion to an equivalent proportion out of 100, then use a calculator to do this.

Further practice

Do these without using a calculator.

2.1   A pupil scores 19 out of 25 in a spelling test and 42 out of 70 marks in a mathematics test. Express these marks as equivalent percentages.

2.2   In Ofsted inspections of a sample of 250 schools, 35 schools were graded as unsatisfactory, and 130 were graded as good, for leadership and management. Express these proportions as percentages. What percentage of schools were graded satisfactory (the only other grade awarded)?

2.3   Three primary schools reported the proportions of their Year 2 pupils achieving level 2 or above for reading as follows:

School P $\frac{3}{5}$ of the pupils achieved level 2 or above

School Q 74% of the pupils achieved level 2 or above

School R   36 out of 45 pupils achieved level 2 or above

Put these proportions in order from the highest to the lowest.

Check-Up

3

Decimals and percentages

a) A primary school calculates the average (mean) National Curriculum level for the core subjects for their pupils at age 11 to be as follows: English, 4.3; mathematics, 4.195; science, 4.28. Arrange these in order from the lowest to the highest.

b) In a secondary school, the proportions of Year 9 pupils achieving level 5 or above in the Key Stage 3 tests last year were 0.76 for mathematics, 0.8 for science and 0.675 for English. Without using a calculator, express these proportions as percentages.

Answers to check-up 3

a) 4.195 (mathematics), 4.28 (science), 4.3 (English).

b) 76% for mathematics, 80% for science, 67.5% for English.

Discussion and explanation of check-up 3

(a) To compare a set of numbers written in decimal notation (such as, 4.3, 4.195, 4.28) if can be helpful to rewrite them (in your head) with the same number of figures after the decimal point. Since one of the numbers in this set has three figures after the decimal point, I might think of them as: 4.300, 4.195 and 4.280. This helps to put them in order: 4.195, 4.280, 4.300. The inclusion of extra zeros after the last figure after a decimal point does not change the value of the number. So, for example, 4.28 means 4 units, 2 tenths and 8 hundredths; and 4.280 means 4 units, 2 tenths, 8 hundredths and no thousands. These are clearly the same. Note that you can mislead yourself by thinking that 4.28 is smaller than 4.195, for example, because 28 is smaller than 195. The misunderstanding here is not to realise that the 28 means '28 hundredths', whereas the 195 means '195 thousandths'. It is also helful to think of the position of these number on a number line diagram, as below. Notice that 4.28 comes between 4.2 and 4.3, and that 4.195 comes between 4.19 and 4.20 (which is also written as 4.2).

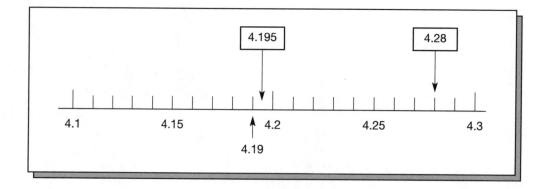

(b) The decimal number 0.76 means 7 tenths and 6 hundredths, or 70 hundredths + 6 hundredths, which is 76 hundredths. Another way of writing 76 hundredths is 76%. So, it is really very easy to convert a decimal number with two figures after the decimal point to a percentage, and *vice versa*: 0.76 = 76%, 0.57 = 57%, 0.40 = 40%, 0.04 = 4%, and so on.

If there is just one figure after the decimal point, then just mentally include an extra zero. For example, 0.8 = 0.80 = 80%. Similarly, 0.2 = 20%, 0.4 = 40% and so on. If there are more than two figures after the decimal point, because it's the first two that tell you how many hundredths you have, you move them so they are in front of the decimal point, as follows: 0.675 = 67.5%. Here are some other examples: 0.045 = 04.5% = 4.5%, 0.1234 = 12.34%, 0.9005 = 90.05%.

Sometimes percentages greater than 100% are used. These can also be written as decimals. Here are some examples: 125% = 1.25, 117.5% = 1.175, 250% = 2.5.

See also...

Check-up 10: Fractions to decimals and vice versa

Summary of key ideas

◆   To compare a set of numbers written in decimal notation it can be helped to rewrite them with the same number of figures after the decimal point.

◆   It is helpful to visualise numbers written in decimal notation in terms of their position on a number line.

◆   To change a decimal number to a percentage, move the digits two places to the left, relative to the decimal point; for example, 0.46 = 46%, 0.175 = 17.5%

◆   To change a percentage to a decimal number, move the digits two places to the right, relative to the decimal point; for example, 99% = 0.99, 150% = 1.50 or 1.5.

Further practice

3.1   A pupil labels some points on a number line in order, as follows: 1.7, 1.8, 1.9, 1.10, ... what is the error here?

3.2   A school's target is that the proportion of pupils absent each day should be less than 0.08. On which of the following days do they *not* achieve the target? The numbers in brackets are the proportions of pupils absent.

Monday (0.075), Tuesday (0.1), Wednesday (0.09), Thursday (0.079), Friday (0.009)

3.3   Without using a calculator, write the proportions given in the previous question as percentages.

Check-Up

4

Understanding data presented in tables

A primary school completed the following table using data provided by the DfES for national results and their own results in the Key Stage 2 science test.

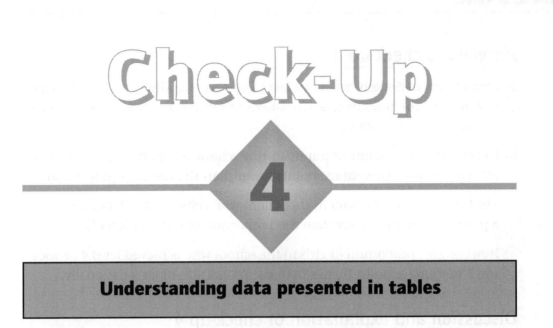

Percentages of pupils attaining level 4 or above in the Key Stage 2 science test.

	National results	School results
All	69	65
Boys	70	62
Girls	68	69

a) What information is represented by the 68 in this table? What is represented by the 62?

b) How well did the pupils in this school do in the science test compared to national results?

Answers to check-up 4

a) 68% of girls nationally achieved level 5 or above in the Key Stage 2 science test. 62% of the boys in this school who took the Key Stage 2 science test achieved level 4 or above.

b) Overall, the proportion of pupils in this school achieving level 4 or above for science was 4 percentage points lower than the national proportion.

The proportion of the boys in the school who achieved level 4 or above was 8 percentage points lower than the proportion of boys nationally.

However, the proportion of girls in the school who achieved level 4 or above was 1 percentage point higher than the proportion of girls nationally.

Discussion and explanation of check-up 4

A table like the one in this check-up question is made up of *rows* and *columns*. A row and a column intersect in a *cell*. The data written in a cell can be either *numbers* or *labels*.

The strategy for reading tables like this is first to be quite clear about what is being measured by the numbers written in the various cells. Technically, we could call this the *variable* and the numbers in the cells are values of the variable. In this case, the variable is 'the percentage of pupils achieving level 4 or above in the Key Stage 2 science test'. We can find this in the caption above the table. The table therefore provides us with the values of this variable for different groups of pupils. So, when we see the number 68 in the table it means 68% of some set of pupils achieved level 4 or above in this test. Then we look at the labels that act as headings for the rows and columns to identify quite clearly and specifically to what each row and each column refers. In this case, for example, the column headed 'National results' refers to the results obtained by pupils from all schools nationally; the column headed 'School results' refers to the results obtained by pupils in this particular school. The rows clearly distinguish between 'all pupils', 'boys' and 'girls'. We can then be quite clear about what each cell refers to. For example, where the 'National results' column meets the 'Girls' row we will find the percentage of girls in all schools nationally who achieved level 4 or above in the Key Stage 2 science test (68%).

Tables like this can be particularly confusing when some of the labels are themselves numbers or percentages. Further Practice question 4.1 is an example of this.

See also…

Check-up 5: Two-way tables for comparing two sets of data

Check-up 39: Increasing or decreasing by a percentage

Summary of key ideas

◆   A table consists of rows and columns, intersecting in cells.

◆   The data written in a cell can be either numbers or labels.

◆   The numbers are usually values of a variable.

◆   To interpret a table, first identify clearly the variable that is being measured by the numbers in the table (usually from the caption).

◆   Then articulate specifically (from the labels) what the rows and columns, and hence the cells, refer to.

Further practice

4.1   The table below provides national data for pupil attendance in secondary schools for two consecutive academic years.

Percentages of secondary schools achieving various attendance rates

Attendance rates...	50–89%	90–91%	92–93%	94–95%	96–97%	98–100%
Year 1	5.2	3.5	17.6	45.0	19.6	9.1
Year 2	6.3	4.1	18.2	43.3	17.9	10.2

a) What is the variable of which the numbers in the cells in this table (5.2, 6.3, 3.5, etc.) are values?

b) What do the labels heading the columns (50–89%, 90–91%, etc.) refer to?

c) What information is represented by the 17.6 in the cell in the middle of the table?

d) What percentage of secondary schools achieved attendance rates in the range 98–100% in Year 2? How did this compare with Year 1?

e) For schools with attendance rates less than 90%, Ofsted Inspectors are required to investigate any relationship between the school's examination results and pupil attendance. To what percentage of secondary schools did this apply in Year 1 and in Year 2?

Check-Up

5

Two-way tables for comparing two sets of data

The following two-way table shows the relationship between GCSE mathematics and English language grades for a Year 11 cohort in a secondary school.

Mathematics

English Language	A*	A	B	C	D	E	F	G	U	X	Totals
A*	2		0	0	0	0	0	0	0	0	3
A	4	4	3	2	0	0	0	0	0	0	13
B	2	3	9	5	1	0	0	0	0	0	20
C	0	1	8	13	2	2	0	0	0	0	
D	0	0	6	9	8	2	2	0	0	0	27
E	0	0	2	5	2	4	1	0	1	0	15
F	0	0	0	1	1	3	2	0	0	0	7
G	0	0	0	0	0	0	0	1	0	0	1
U	0	0	0	0	0	0	0	0	1	1	2
X	0	0	0	0	0	0	0	0	0	0	0
Totals	8	9		35	14	11	5	1	2	1	114

a) Fill in the three missing numbers in the table.

b) How many pupils were there in the cohort?

c) Of the pupils who were graded C for English language, how many achieved the same grade for mathematics? How many achieved a higher grade? How many a lower grade?

Answers to check-up 5

a) From left to right, the missing numbers are 1, 28 and 26.

b) 114 pupils.

c) 13 the same grade; 9 higher; 4 lower.

Discussion and explanation of check-up 5

The variable of which the numbers in this table are values is simply the number of pupils achieving various grades. For example, 5 pupils achieved grade E for English language and grade C for mathematics. Reading down the column headed B for mathematics, we can see how many of the pupils who achieved grade B for this subject achieved various grades for English language: 0, 3, 9, 8, 6, 2, 0, 0, 0, 0, respectively for grades A*, A, B, C, D, E, F, G, U and X. The sum of these numbers (28) is the total number of pupils who achieved grade B for mathematics. This is the number that goes in the cell at the bottom of the column, in the row labelled 'totals'. The missing number in the A* row for English language must be 1 in order to give 3 as the total for that row. Reading along the C row for English language, we see that, of the pupils who achieved grade C for this subject, none of them was graded A* for mathematics, 1 was graded A, 8 graded B, 13 graded C, 2 graded D, and 2 graded E. The sum of these, written in the cell at the end of the row, in the column headed 'totals', is 26. This means that in total, 26 pupils were graded C for English language.

Notice that the total number of pupils in the cohort (114) is shown in the cell in the bottom right-hand corner. This can be found by summing either the row-totals or the column-totals. You should always check that these give the same answer. If they do not, then there must be an error somewhere in the table.

Arranding two sets of data in a two-way table like this is a useful device for making comparisons between them. The diagonal from top-left to bottom-right shows how many pupils achieved the same grades for the two subjects. This is a useful starting point for interpreting this particular table. A quick glance at the data above and below this diagonal reveals that there are more pupils below it than above it. This indicates a tendency for pupils in this cohort to achieve lower grades in English language than in mathematics. For example, of those graded C for English, 9 achieved higher grades for mathematics (8 grade B and a grade A), whereas only 4 achieved lower grades (2 grade E and 2 grade F).

See also...

Check-up 4: Understanding data presented in tables

Check-up 50: Reading scatter graphs

Summary of key ideas

◆ Arranging two sets of data in a two-way table is a useful device for making comparisons between the two sets.

◆ If the table includes totals of the numbers in the rows and columns, then the overall total can be obtained either by adding the row-totals or the column-totals.

Further practice

5.1   As part of her drive to improve attendance rates, a headteacher used the following two-way table to investigate the relationship between pupils' travelling time to school and the number of days they were absent in one particular term.

	Journey time in minutes				
	1–15	16–30	31–45	46–60	Totals
0–4	102	79	18	6	205
5–9	51	13	6	4	
10–14	15	4	3	0	22
15–19	1	0	0	0	1
Totals	169	96	27	10	302

Number of days absent (row label, left side)

a) Fill in the missing number. What does this represent?

b) How many pupils with a journey time greater than 30 minutes were absent for 10 or more days? And how many for less than 10 days?

c) How many pupils with a journey time of 30 minutes or less were absent for 10 or more days? And how many for less than 10 days?

d) Does the data here support the headteacher's hunch that pupils with longer journey times tend to have more absences?

Check-Up

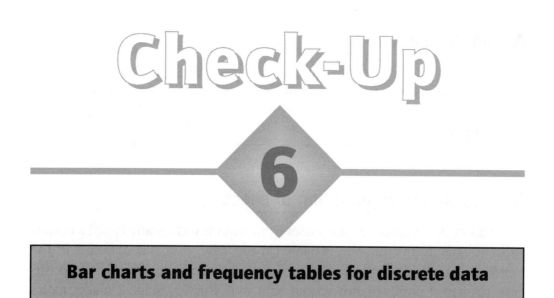

6

Bar charts and frequency tables for discrete data

The assessment coordinator in a primary school enters the numbers of pupils achieving various levels in the Key Stage 2 mathematics test into an Excel worksheet and generates the bar chart shown.

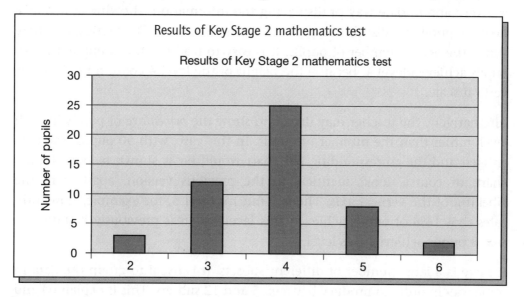

Use the bar chart to reconstruct the data that gave rise to it. Enter the data into this frequency table:

Level					
No. of pupils					

Answer to check-up 6

Level	2	3	4	5	6
No. of pupils	3	12	25	8	2

Discussion and explanation of check-up 6

The data in this frequency table arises from what is technically called a *discrete variable*. This means that the variable (in this case, the level obtained in the Key Stage 2 mathematics test) divides the population being considered (in this case, the set of pupils in this school who took the Key Stage 2 mathematics test) into a number of *discrete* (separate) subsets. The *values* of the variable (2, 3, 4, 5, 6) are shown along the horizontal axis. In this example the subsets produced are the pupils achieving level 2, those achieving level 3, and so on. Each pupil belongs to one and only one subset. In an example like this, a bar chart is a very appropriate way of displaying the information, showing at a glance how the pupils are distributed across the various subsets. The vertical axis here shows the actual number of pupils. It is easy to read off, for example, that 25 pupils achieved level 4, because the height of the level 4 column is 25 on the vertical scale.

Alternatively, the teacher may decide to show the *percentage* of pupils in each level, rather than the number of pupils. In this case, with 50 pupils, the data entered and the corresponding bar chart would be as shown below. The bar chart, of course, looks identical to the previous version, apart from the labelling of the vertical axis. The column for level 5, for example, now indicates that 16% of pupils achieved this level, whereas previously it indicated that 8 pupils achieved this level.

If there is a large number of different subsets, it is usual to group the data in some way in order to produce between 5 and 12 subsets. This is explained and discussed in Check-up 7.

Level	2	3	4	5	6
% of pupils	6	24	50	16	4

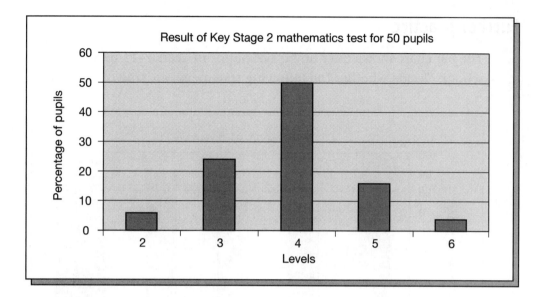

See also...

Check-up 7: Bar charts for grouped discrete data

Check-up 8: Bar charts for continuous data

Check-up 53: Interpreting pie charts

Summary of key ideas

◆   A bar chart is usually an appropriate way of displaying pictorially a set of data arising from a discrete variable.

◆   A discrete variable divides a population into a number of discrete (separate) subsets, with each individual in the population belonging to one and only one subset.

◆   The values of the variable are usually shown on the horizontal axis.

◆   The height of a column, shown by the scale on the vertical axis, usually represents the frequency, that is the number of individuals in the various subsets.

◆   The frequencies can also be expressed as percentages of the population.

Further practice

6.1   The bar chart shows the numbers of pupils in Years 7–11 in a secondary school. Decide whether the following statements are true or false.

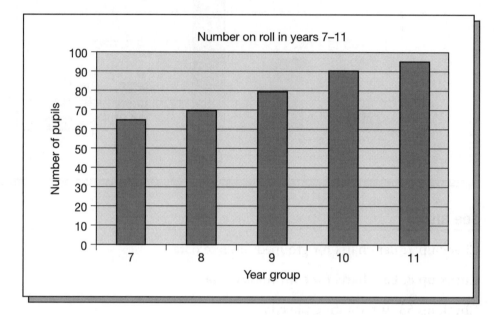

a) The year with the most pupils is Year 11.

b) Year 11 has 10 more pupils than Year 10.

c) There are 400 pupils in total in Years 7–11.

d) About 25% of the pupils are in Year 7.

e) The intake to the school has risen gradually over the last five years.

Check-Up

7

Bar charts for grouped discrete data

A teacher recorded the results of a science test (marked out of 80), for a year group of 84 pupils, in an Excel worksheet. This generated the bar chart shown here. Are these statements true or false?

a) The graph shows that the highest mark obtained in the test was 80.

b) 15 pupils achieved marks in the range 41 to 50 inclusive.

c) No pupils scored marks in the range 11 to 30 inclusive.

d) 30 pupils scored more than 60 marks out of 80.

e) Fewer than 10% of the pupils scored less than half marks.

f) One pupil did very much worse than all the rest.

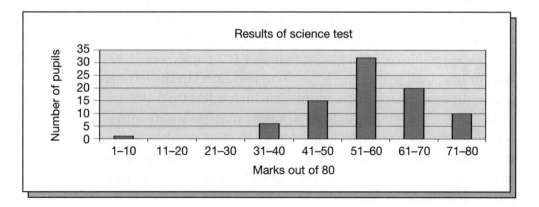

Answer to check-up 7

a) False.   b) True.   c) True.   d) True.   e) True.   f) True.

Discussion and explanation of check-up 7

The variable in this example is simply the mark out of 80 achieved by pupils in the science test. This is a discrete variable, since it separates the set of pupils into separate subsets, i.e. those with scores of 0, 1, 2, 3, 4, 5, 6, and so on, up to 80. But clearly there are too many of these subsets to represent in a bar chart. The resulting diagram would convey nothing that you could not see better by just looking at the marks themselves. In a case like this, where the variable takes numerous values, it is usual to group the values into intervals covering a range of values. The width of each interval should normally be the same. In this example it was decided to go for intervals covering a range of 10 marks, thus producing eight possible subsets across the whole range of marks obtained by the pupils: 1–10, 11–20, 21–30, and so on. The size of the intervals should be chosen to produce from five to twelve subsets: fewer than five and too much information is lost, more than twelve and too much detail is retained for the graph to be of any use.

So in the graph, each column represents the number of pupils whose marks fall within the given range. The graph loses the precise details of the individual marks, so, for example, we can read off that 10 pupils scored from 71 to 80, but we do not know if anyone actually scored 80. Notice that it is important in covering the whole range to include in the graph any intervals in which there were no pupils. The absence of pupils scoring in the intervals 11–20 and 21–30 is significant information, given the fact that one pupil scored a mark in the range 1–10. This pupil's poor result compared with the rest is immediately communicated by the pictorial representation of the data in the bar chart. You can also see at a glance that very few pupils scored 40 marks or less, with only a small part of the population appearing in the left-hand half of the graph. (In fact, the total here is only 7, which is less than 10% of the whole set of 84 pupils.) The whole purpose of putting numerical data into graphical form is to make it possible to take in at a glance the way the data is distributed across the range of possible values. If the teacher looking at this graph can get an immediate impression of how the pupils have done on the test, then the bar chart has fulfilled its purpose.

See also...

Check-up 8: Bar charts for continuous data

Check-up 43: Modes

Summary of key ideas

◆ If a set of numerical data contains numerous different values of a discrete variable then it is often useful to group the data into intervals before representing it in a bar chart.

◆ The intervals should be of equal width, should be chosen to cover the whole range, and should produce from five to twelve subsets.

◆ In a bar chart for grouped discrete data, the height of a column indicates the frequency of values that fall within the interval shown.

Further practice

7.1   Which of the following sets of data would probably need to be grouped into intervals before representing it in a bar chart:

a) the reading ages of the pupils in a Year 2 class, expressed in years and months (e.g. 5.2, 5.11, 7.2)

b) the number of GCSE subjects passed at grade C or above by pupils in a Year 11 class

c) the total point score for pupils in a Year 11 class based on their GCSE/GNVQ grades for all subjects (where grade G = 1 point, F = 2 points, and so on).

7.2   A local education authority, concerned about the variation in class size across the LEA, produced this bar chart.

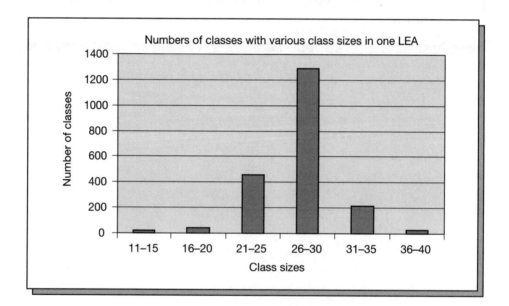

a) About how many classes have over 35 pupils?

b) About how many classes have 20 or fewer pupils?

c) Approximately how many classes in total are represented here?

d) The LEA's target is to have from 26 to 30 pupils in 75% or more of their classes; have they achieved this?

Check-Up

8

The pupil–teacher ratio (PTR) for a school is calculated by dividing the number of pupils by the number of teachers. The bar chart shows the distribution of PTRs across all the primary schools in one LEA. To process the data the PTRs have been rounded to one decimal place.

a) What is the PTR for a school with 345 pupils and 17 teachers?

b) Approximately, for what percentage of schools is the PTR in the range 20.0–24.9?

c) Approximately, for what percentage of schools is the PTR 25 or greater?

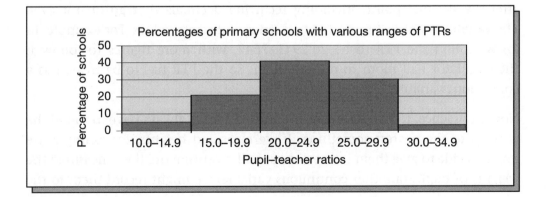

Percentages of primary schools with various ranges of PTRs

Answers to check-up 8

a) 20.294117647… (using a calculator), which rounds to 20.3.

b) About 41%.

c) About 33%.

Discussion and explanation of check-up 8

For (a), on my calculator, I enter 345 ÷ 17 =, to find the PTR for 345 pupils and 17 teachers. This gives the result 20.294117647. Because this is nearer to 20.3 than 20.2, when we round it to one decimal place we give it as 20.3. The answer for (b) is obtained by reading off on the vertical axis the approximate height of the column labelled '20.0–24.9'. For (c) we have to add the percentages for '25.0–29.9' (about 30%) and for '30.0–34.9' (about 3%), giving 33% in total.

In Check-ups 6 and 7 we looked at displaying data from a frequency table where the variable could only take a certain number of separate (discrete) values. For example, Key Stage 2 mathematics test levels could only be whole numbers, namely, 1, 2, 3, 4, 5 and 6. Reading ages for a Year 2 class could only take values such as 5.1, 5.2, 5.3, 5.4, and so on. Contrast these with a variable like the height of pupils in a school. This could lie anywhere on a continuum of values from the minimum height to the maximum height. A growing pupil's height does not suddenly jump from 145.6 cm to 145.7 cm, for example. It increases continuously through all the values in between. For example, at one moment the pupil's height is presumably 145.654321 cm, even though we would not be able to measure it to that degree of precision. Such a variable is said to be *continuous*. In the example in Check-up 8, the variable could theoretically take thousands of different values, with any number of figures after the decimal point, including recurring decimals that go on for ever. The variable is not just restricted to a series of discrete values. For example, in (a) we found the PTR to be 20.294117647, with more figures to follow if the calculator had room to display them. So the PTR has to be treated as a continuous variable.

Now, in practice, to handle a continuous variable we always have to round the answers to the nearest something. If we measured heights, for example, we might decide to give them to the nearest half-a-centimetre. If we measured the weights of pupils (another continuous variable) we might record them to the nearest 100 grams. In this check-up, each PTR has been rounded to one decimal place. Once you have done this, you have effectively turned it into a discrete variable – and it is handled in exactly the same way as the data in Check-up 7, grouping it into appropriately sized intervals. But just to indicate that the original data was continuous in nature, the convention is usually to draw the bar chart with no gaps between the columns, as has been done here.

See also...

Check-up 19: Rounding answers

Summary of key ideas

◆   A continuous variable (like the height of pupils in a school) is one that can take any value on a continuum and is not restricted to a series of discrete values.

◆   In practice, because continuous data always has to be rounded to the nearest something (e.g. to one decimal place), it could be grouped and handled in the same way as grouped discrete data.

◆   To indicate that the data came from a continuous variable, when it is represented in a bar chart the columns should be drawn without any gaps between them.

Further practice

8.1   Decide which of these variables are continuous:

a) the number of children in the families of pupils in a school

b) the times taken by pupils in a Year 7 group to run 100 metres

c) the number of A-level passes obtained by pupils in an A-level cohort

d) the ratio of girth (waist-size) to height for the 45 members of a school staff (this is called the index of rotundity!).

8.2   For the examples in 8.1 that are continuous variables, decide how you would round the data to the nearest something and then how you would group the data in intervals for display in a bar chart.

Check-Up

9

Finding a fraction of a quantity

a) Two-thirds ($\frac{2}{3}$) of the 480 pupils in a school are of non-white ethnicity. Without using a calculator, find how many pupils this is.

b) One supplier lists a computer as costing £990 but offers schools three-tenths ($\frac{3}{10}$) off the list price. A second store prices the same computer at £1200 but offers two-fifths ($\frac{2}{5}$) off the price. Without using a calculator, decide which is cheaper.

c) Five-twelfths ($\frac{5}{12}$) of the science departmental budget of £1900 can be spent on textbooks. Use a calculator to find how much this is.

Answers to check-up 9

a) 320 pupils.

b) The first (£693) is cheaper than the second (£720).

c) About £790.

Discussion and explanation of check-up 9

The bottom number in a fraction is called the *denominator*. It tells you into how many equal parts the whole quantity is to be divided. The top number is called the *numerator*. This tells you how many of these parts are required. So, the fraction $\frac{2}{3}$ in example (a) is an instruction to divide the 480 into three equal parts and then to take two of these parts. You should be able to do this mentally, without using a formal written method. First you calculate one-third of 480, which is 160. Then you multiply this by 2 to obtain two-thirds, which is 320 pupils.

In practice, people do sometimes express proportions using simple fractions like $\frac{2}{3}$, $\frac{3}{10}$ and $\frac{2}{5}$. However, it is much more common – and more sensible – to express them using percentages, as in Check-ups 1 and 2. It is certainly rare that we will hear people actually use fractions like $\frac{5}{12}$ in real life! So, to be quite honest, examples (b) and (c) here are the kinds of pointless, contrived questions that people get asked in numeracy tests rather than the kinds of statements that you will really encounter in your professional life as a teacher.

So, this is how you might do example (b). To find $\frac{3}{10}$ of £990, first find one-tenth (£99) and then multiply by three ($3 \times £99 = 3 \times £100 - £3 = £300 - £3 = £297$). Subtract this £297 from the list price to get the offer price of £693. Alternatively, you could say that '$\frac{3}{10}$ off' means that the offer price will be $\frac{7}{10}$ of the list price and simply calculate $\frac{7}{10}$ of £990 directly: £990 ÷ 10 × 7 = £693. Similarly, for the second supplier, you could find one-fifth of £1200 (£240), double this to get two-fifths and subtract this from the £1200. Alternatively, you could just calculate three-fifths of £1200 directly: £1200 ÷ 5 × 3 = £720.

In example (c), because the denominator (12) does not divide easily into the given quantity (£1900), it might make most sense to use a calculator to divide by 12 and multiply by 5. The key sequence on the calculator is '1900 ÷ 12 × 5 =' The basic four-function calculator on the computer that I am using at the moment gives the answer as 791.66666667. This represents just over £790. I am assuming that, in this context, working to the nearest £10 would be a reasonable choice.

See also...

Check-up 19: Rounding answers

Check-up 10: Fractions to decimals and vice versa

Check-up 11: Expressing a percentage in fraction notation

Summary of key ideas

◆ To find the fraction $\frac{a}{b}$ of a quantity, divide by b (the denominator) and multiply by a (the numerator).

◆ If b divides exactly and easily into the given quantity you should be able to handle this mentally (e.g. $\frac{4}{5}$ of £300).

◆ Otherwise (e.g. $\frac{7}{12}$ of £3020), use a calculator, rounding the calculator answer appropriately.

Further practice

9.1 A teacher walks into the staff room and says, 'Four-sevenths of my class of 28 pupils are girls. How many are boys?' What would you reply?

9.2 Precisely 2 in 9 of the 144 trainees on a primary PGCE course are male. How many is this? (Do not use a calculator.)

9.3 The Value Added Tax payable on a television is $\frac{7}{40}$ of the catalogue price of £649.99. Use a calculator to find how much VAT is payable.

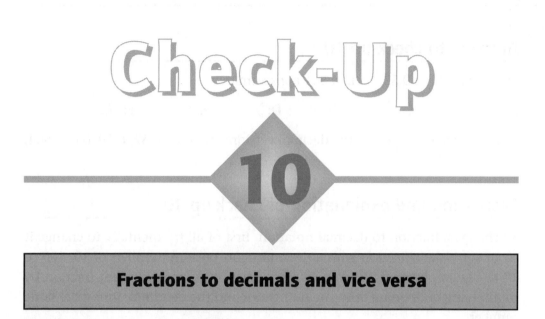

Check-Up

10

Fractions to decimals and vice versa

Six schools choose to report the proportions of their Year 11 pupils obtaining 5 or more GCSE passes at grade C or above in a variety of ways:

School A: three-fifths of the pupils   School B: 0.75 of the pupils

School C: 13 pupils in every 25   School D: 0.625 of the pupils

School E: 119 pupils out of 197   School F: 0.59 of the pupils

a) Express the proportions for A, C and E in decimal notation. (Only use a calculator if necessary.)

b) Express all the proportions in fraction notation.

c) Which notation is the easier to use to put these proportions in order of size?

Answers to check-up 10

a) A: 0.6.   C: 0.52.   E: 0.604 approximately.

b) A: $\frac{3}{5}$ B: $\frac{3}{4}$ C: $\frac{13}{25}$ D: $\frac{5}{8}$ E: $\frac{119}{197}$ F: $\frac{59}{100}$.

c) It is much easier to put the decimal versions in order: 0.52, 0.59, 0.6, 0.604, 0.625, 0.75.

Discussion and explanation of check-up 10

To change a fraction to decimal notation, first of all try mentally to change it to an equivalent fraction with a denominator (bottom number) of 10, 100 or 1000 – i.e. a power of 10. You change a fraction to an equivalent fraction by multiplying or dividing both the numerator and the denominator by the same number.

School A: three-fifths = $\frac{3}{5}$ = $\frac{6}{10}$ (multiplying top and bottom by 2) = 0.6 (because 0.6 = 6 tenths).

School C: 13 in every 25 = $\frac{13}{25}$ = $\frac{52}{100}$ (multiplying top and bottom by 4) = 0.52 (because 0.52 = 52 hundredths).

The 119 out of 197 for School E cannot be done in this way, because there is no obvious, simple way of getting from 197 to a power of 10. In this case the fraction is changed to decimal notation simply by dividing the numerator by the denominator, using a calculator: 119 ÷ 197 = 0.60406091371. This can then be rounded to an appropriate number of figures after the decimal point.

To change from decimal notation to fraction notation, express the decimal as so many tenths, hundredths or thousandths, depending on whether there are one, two or three figures after the decimal point. (It is unlikely that there would be any reason to express in fraction notation a decimal number with more than three figures after the point.) Then divide top and bottom by whatever *factors* they have in common to obtain the simplest equivalent fraction – this process is called *cancelling*. For example, 0.8 = $\frac{8}{10}$ = $\frac{4}{5}$ (cancelling 2, which is a factor of both 8 and 10).

School B: 0.75 = $\frac{75}{100}$ = $\frac{3}{4}$ (cancelling 25, which is a factor of both 75 and 100).

School D: 0.625 = $\frac{625}{1000}$ = $\frac{125}{200}$ (cancelling 5) = $\frac{5}{8}$ (cancelling 25).

School F: $0.59 = \frac{59}{100}$ (this cannot be simplified; 59 and 100 have no common factors).

It is usually much easier to compare proportions expressed in decimal notation (or as percentages) than in fraction notation. I cannot compare $\frac{3}{5}$ and $\frac{119}{197}$ at a glance, but I can immediately see that 0.6 is less than 0.604 (or that 60% is less than 60.4%).

See also...

Check-up 3: Decimals and percentages

Check-up 11: Expressing a percentage in fraction notation

Check-up 19: Rounding answers

Summary of key ideas

◆   To change a fraction to an equivalent fraction, multiply or divide both the numerator and the denominator by the same number.

◆   Dividing both numerator and denominator by a common factor is called *cancelling*.

◆   To change a fraction to decimal notation, first of all try mentally to change it to an equivalent fraction with a denominator of 10, 100 or 1000.

◆   To change from decimal to fraction notation, express the decimal as tenths, hundredths or thousandths, depending on the number of figures after the decimal point, and then cancel as much as possible.

◆   It is easier to compare proportions expressed in decimal notation or as percentages than in fraction notation.

Further practice

10.1 Without recourse to a calculator, express the following in decimal notation, compare the answers with Further Practice question 1.1 (from Check-up 1), and then commit them all to memory!

$$\frac{1}{10}, \frac{3}{10}, \frac{7}{10}, \frac{9}{10}, \frac{1}{5}, \frac{2}{5}, \frac{3}{5}, \frac{4}{5}, \frac{1}{8}, \frac{3}{8}, \frac{5}{8}, \frac{7}{8}, \frac{1}{20}, \frac{3}{20}, \frac{7}{20}, \frac{9}{20}$$

10.2 Change (a) 0.175 and (b) 0.007 to fraction notation.

10.3 One subject department in a secondary school has spent four-sevenths of their equipment budget; another has spent £879 out of £1500. Using a calculator, decide which has spent the larger proportion of their budget.

Check-Up

11

Expressing a percentage in fraction notation

Data from the DfES about the proportions of secondary schools with various percentages of pupils for whom English is an additional language is given in this table.

% of pupils for whom English is an additional language	% of total schools
20% and over	10%
10–19%	4%
5–9%	5%
1–4%	18%
below 1%	63%

a) Rewrite each of the percentages given in the right-hand column using fraction notation.

b) A total of 1042 secondary schools out of 18224 had 40% and over pupils in this category. Approximately what percentage of schools is this (to the nearest 1%)? Now express this result in fraction notation.

Answers to check-up 11

a) $10\% = \frac{1}{10}$ $4\% = \frac{1}{25}$ $5\% = \frac{1}{20}$ $18\% = \frac{9}{50}$ $63\% = \frac{63}{100}$.

b) $1042 \div 18224 = 0.05717734855 = 0.06$ approximately $= 6\% = \frac{3}{50}$.

Discussion and explanation of check-up 11

This check-up focuses on the reverse process of expressing proportions as percentages discussed in Check-ups 1, 2 and 18.

Most people know that 10% is also $\frac{1}{10}$ (one-tenth). This is because 10% means '10 in 100', which is equivalent to '1 in 10'. But, of course, this is a special case. For example, 4% is not '1 in 4' and 6% is not $\frac{1}{6}$!

The proportion 4% is '4 in 100', which, expressed in fraction notation, is $\frac{4}{100}$. Cancelling 4, because this is a factor of both 4 and 100, this simplifies to $\frac{1}{25}$.

Similarly, $5\% = \frac{5}{100} = \frac{1}{20}$ (cancelling 5) and $18\% = \frac{18}{100} = \frac{9}{50}$ (cancelling 2).

These proportions could also be expressed as '1 in 20' and '9 in 50'.

The proportion 63% is '63 in 100'. Written in fraction notation this would be $\frac{63}{100}$. This cannot be simplified further because 63 and 100 have no factors in common.

In example (b) the proportion 1042 out of 18224 is found to be equal to the decimal number 0.05717734855, using a calculator (see Check-up 18). Using the ideas in Check-up 3, moving the figures two places to the left, this is equivalent to 5.717734855%. This is approximately 6% to the nearest whole percent. Then, $6\% = \frac{6}{100} = \frac{3}{50}$ (cancelling 2). So we could say that 'about 6 schools in 100' or 'about 3 schools in 50' have 40% or more pupils with English as an additional language.

As was encouraged in Check-up 1, you should be able to recall instantly common equivalences between fractions and percentages, such as $20\% = \frac{1}{5}$, $5\% = \frac{1}{20}$ and $25\% = \frac{1}{4}$.

See also...

Check-up 18: Using a calculator to express a proportion as a percentage

Check-up 19: Rounding answers

Summary of key ideas

◆   A proportion can be expressed as a percentage, in decimal notation or in fraction notation.

◆   For example, these all represent the same proportion: '45 in 100', 45%, 0.45, $\frac{45}{100}$.

◆   The fraction version may then be simplified by cancelling common factors: for example, $\frac{45}{100} = \frac{9}{20}$ (cancelling 5).

Further practice

% of pupils eligible for FSM	% of schools
more than 50%	5%
36–50%	10%
21–35%	18%
9–20%	30%
8% and below	37%

11.1 The table shows the percentages of all primary schools with Key Stage 2 pupils that have various proportions of pupils known to be eligible for free schools meals (FSM). Express in fraction notation all the percentages given in the right-hand column.

11.2 One rate of Value-Added Tax (VAT) is 17.5% (or $17\frac{1}{2}$%). Express this as a fraction.

11.3 A secondary school reports that about $87\frac{1}{2}$% of the Year 11 pupils are going on to sixth form studies and only $12\frac{1}{2}$% are not. Express these statements using fraction notation. Because together they represent the whole cohort, the sum of the two percentages here must be 100%. What must be the sum of the two fractions?

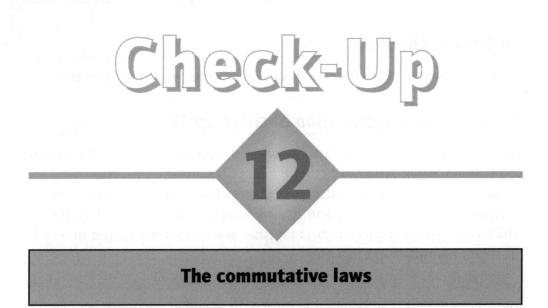

Check-Up

12

The commutative laws

This check-up and the following two are designed to make explicit some fundamental laws of arithmetic. Whatever the numbers *a* and *b*,

a)   is it always true, sometimes true, or never true that $a + b = b + a$?

b)   is it always true, sometimes true, or never true that $a - b = b - a$?

c)   is it always true, sometimes true, or never true that $ab = ba$?

d)   is it always true, sometimes true, or never true that $a \div b = b \div a$?

Answers to check-up 12

a) Always true.   b) Sometimes true. c) Always true.   d) Sometimes true.

Discussion and explanation of check-up 12

The statements in (a) and (c) are known as the *commutative laws* of addition and multiplication. Remember that *ab* in algebraic notation is a shorthand for '*a* multiplied by *b*'. The generalisations that $a + b = b + a$ and $ab = ba$, whatever numbers are chosen for *a* and *b*, state simply that it does not matter in which order you add two numbers together and it does not matter in which order you multiply them together.

For example, using the commutative law of addition we could change 3 + 8999 into 8999 + 3. This is probably what most of us would do mentally, because it's easier to start at 8999 and count on by 3 (to get 9002) than to start at 3 and count on by 8999! The commutative law of multiplication allows us, for example, to change '5 sevens' into '7 fives'. Most people find it is easier to visualise counting in fives than in sevens. If the desks in your classroom were arranged in 5 rows of 7, you could also think of them as 7 rows of 5.

Here's a useful application of the commutative law of multiplication using percentages. Say you have to calculate 28% of £25. Well, because multiplication is commutative, you would get the same result if you calculate 25% of £28, which is very easy to do mentally ($\frac{1}{4}$ of £28 = £7).

Mathematicians say that addition and multiplication are *commutative*. Subtraction and division are not. With subtraction, it matters in what order the numbers are written down. '8 – 3' (= 5) is not the same thing as '3 – 8' (= -5). Think of subtraction here as counting back along a number line: '3 - 8' would take you down to –5. (This is like the temperature starting at 3°C, then falling by 8°.) With division, '12 ÷ 3' and '3 ÷ 12' are certainly not interchangeable: 12 ÷ 3 = 4, but 3 ÷ 12 = $\frac{1}{4}$ or 0.25. So, if you have a difficult division calculation to do, such as finding the price per gram of 1450 grams of some substance costing £27.99, you have to think carefully about the order in which you enter the numbers on the calculator. In this example, to find the price per gram, you divide the price by the weight: 27.99 ÷ 1450 = 0.0193034 = 0.02 approximately, giving £0.02 or 2p per gram.

The only occasions when $a - b = b - a$ and $a \div b = b \div a$ are true are when a and b are the same number. For example, $7 - 7 = 7 - 7$ and $42 \div 42 = 42 \div 42$, rather obviously, which is why the answers to (b) and (d) are 'sometimes true'. (There is one further exception in the case of division. We have to exclude the case where a and b are both zero. Any division by zero is meaningless. Try $0 \div 0$ on your calculator: all you will get will be an indication that you have made an error.)

See also...

Check-up 13: The associative laws

Check-up 14: The distributive laws

Summary of key ideas

◆   Addition and multiplication are commutative, which means that it does not matter in what order you add them together or multiply them together.

◆   In algebraic form we say that, for any numbers a and b, $a + b = b + a$ and $ab = ba$.

◆   Subtraction and division are not commutative: $a - b$ is not equal to $b - a$ and $a \div b$ is not equal to $b \div a$ (except when a and b are the same number).

Further practice

12.1 Use the commutativity of multiplication to help calculate mentally: (a) 48% of £75 and (b) 35% of £60.

12.2 On a school skiing holiday, the coach takes 14.5 hours for the 895 km journey. What would you enter on a calculator to find the average speed in kilometres per hour: $14.5 \div 895$ or $895 \div 14.5$?

12.3 True or false?

a) $28 \times 0 = 28$ b) $0 \times 28 = 0$ c) $28 \div 0 = 28$ d) $0 \div 28 = 0$

Check-Up

13

The associative laws

Each pupil in a class of A pupils requires B kilograms of flour for a series of food technology lessons. Flour costs £C per kilogram.

a) What will be the total cost if A = 29, B = 2.5 and C = 0.46?

b) Which of the following formulas gives the total cost in pounds: A × (B × C) or (A × B) × C?

Answers to check-up 13

a) £33.35.   b) Either of the formulas can be used.

Discussion and explanation of check-up 13

To calculate the total cost of the flour required here, you could first calculate the total cost per pupil (B × C) and multiply this by the number of pupils. This would be using the formula A × (B × C). The brackets indicate which bit of the calculation is to be done first. Alternatively, you could first calculate the total amount of flour required for the class (A × B) and then multiply this by the cost per kilogram. This would be using the formula (A × B) × C. Either way you get the same result.

This demonstrates what is called the *associative law* of multiplication: A × (B × C) = (A × B) × C, whatever numbers are chosen for A, B and C. This means that if you have three numbers to be multiplied together, the one in the middle can be 'associated' with either the first number or the last number and you get the same answer. This is very useful in mental calculations. For example, to calculate 4 × (5 × 13) it is much easier to think of it as (4 × 5) × 13, i.e. 20 × 13, which equals 260. So, if I had to calculate 12 × 35 mentally, I would think of the 35 as (5 × 7) and then associate the 5 with the 12 as follows: 12 × 35 = 12 × (5 × 7) = (12 × 5) × 7 = 60 × 7 = 420.

Because A × (B × C) and (A × B) × C are equal, we can just write 'A × B × C' without any brackets, recognising that it does not matter whether we start with the A × B or with the B × C.

When we combine the associative property of multiplication with the commutative law (Check-up 12), the upshot is that we can multiply three (or more) numbers together in any order you like! So, for example, if you had to calculate 25 × (86 × 4) you could rearrange this as 25 × (4 × 86), using the commutative law. Using the associative law, this then becomes (25 × 4) × 86, which is 100 × 86 = 8600.

All this is also true of addition. The associate law of addition is: A + (B + C) = (A + B) + C, allowing us to write just 'A + B + C' to mean either of these. Combined with commutativity, this property allows us to add three (or more) numbers in any order we like: which is probably what you would have done anyway, even if I had not given you this elaborate mathematical explanation!

You will probably have guessed by now that subtraction and division are not associative. These operations are explored in the further practice questions.

See also...

Check-up 21: Mental calculations, multiplication strategies

Check-up 26: Mental calculations, adding lists

Summary of key ideas

◆   Addition is associative.

◆   In algebraic notation: $A + (B + C) = (A + B) + C$, for any numbers A, B and C.

◆   This allows us to write 'A + B + C' to mean either of these.

◆   Multiplication is also associative.

◆   In algebraic notation: $A \times (B \times C) = (A \times B) \times C$, for any numbers A, B and C.

◆   This allows us to write $A \times B \times C$ to mean either of these.

◆   Subtraction and division are not associative.

Further practice

13.1 Confirm that subtraction is not associative by evaluating '30 − (18 − 10)' and '(30 − 18) − 10'. Which of these corresponds to this situation: in a class of 30, the 18 pupils who still have to return their school-home contracts were asked to bring them in on Monday, but 10 of them forgot again; how many contracts were now returned?

13.2 Do two calculations involving the numbers 160, 8 and 4, to demonstrate that division is not associative.

13.3 Use the associative law to calculate mentally the cost of 28 books at £25 each, by thinking of the 28 as 7 × 4.

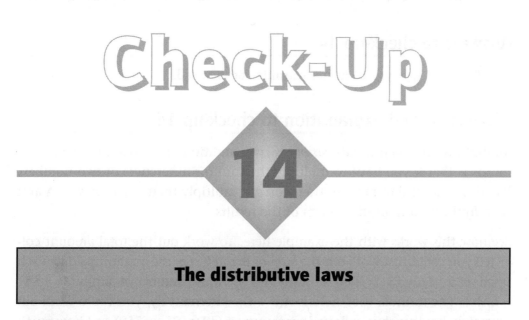

The distributive laws

There are A pupils in a class. The school charges them each £B to cover the cost of transport for a field trip, plus an additional £C to cover other costs.

a) Without a calculator, find the total amount collected if A = 30, B = 25 and C = 6.

b) Which of these formulas gives the total amount collected in pounds: A(B + C) or AB + AC?

Answers to check-up 14

a) £930.   b) Either formula can be used.

Discussion and explanation to check-up 14

Multiplication is said to be *distributive* over addition or subtraction. What this means is that if you have to multiply the sum (or difference) of two numbers B and C by a third number A, then you can multiply them separately by A and then find the sum (or difference) of the results.

See how this works with the example here. To work out the total amount collected you could first work out the sum of B and C, i.e. the amount paid by each pupil (£25 + £6 = £31). Then multiply this by A, the number of pupils (30 × £31 = £930). The formula used here is A(B + C). Alternatively, you could work out separately how much is collected for transport (30 × £25 = £750) and how much is collected for other costs (30 × £6 = £180). Then add these: £750 + £180 = £930. The formula used here is AB + AC. These procedures come to the same result. They always do, whatever numbers are used. Written algebraically, the distributive laws for multiplication state that for any numbers A, B and C: A(B + C) = AB + AC and A(B − C) = AB − AC. Remember that AB is shorthand for 'A multiplied by B', and A(B + C) means 'A multiplied by the sum of B and C'.

These distributive laws are the basis of many approaches to multiplication calculations, both written and mental. For example, if you had to work out the cost of 28 textbooks at £9 each, you might handle the multiplication mentally by splitting the 28 into 20 + 8, like this: 9 × 28 = 9 × (20 + 8) = (9 × 20) + (9 × 8) = 180 + 72 = 252. The multiplication by 9 has been 'distributed' across the sum of 20 and 8. Or, you could rewrite the 28 mentally as 30 − 2, like this: 9 × 28 = 9 × (30 − 2) = (9 × 30) − (9 × 2) = 270 − 18 = 252. This time the multiplication by 9 has been distributed across the difference of 30 and 2.

Division by a number can also be distributed across a sum or difference, giving us these two distributive laws: (B + C) ÷ A = (B ÷ A) + (C ÷ A) and (B − C) ÷ A = (B ÷ A) − (C ÷ A). (Of course, these don't make sense if A = 0.) For example, 171 ÷ 9 could be handled by distributing the division by 9 across the sum of 99 and 72, like this: 171 ÷ 9 = (99 + 72) ÷ 9 = (99 ÷ 9) + (72 ÷ 9) = 11 + 8 = 19. Or, the division by 9 could be distributed across the difference of 180 and 9, like this: 171 ÷ 9 = (180 − 9) ÷ 9 = (180 ÷ 9) − (9 ÷ 9) = 20 − 1 = 19. In both cases, I have chosen to rewrite the 171 in terms of numbers that I can easily divide by 9 (i.e. 99 and 72, 180 and 9).

See also...

Check-up 21: Mental calculations, multiplication strategies

Check-up 22: Mental calculations, division strategies

Summary of key ideas

◆ Multiplication is said to be *distributive* over addition or subtraction.

◆ This means that to multiply the sum (or difference) of two numbers by something you can multiply them separately and then find the sum (or difference) of the results.

◆ Algebraically, for any numbers A, B and C:
$A(B + C) = AB + AC$, and $A(B - C) = AB - AC$.

◆ Division by a number is also distributive across addition and subtraction.

◆ Algebraically, for any numbers A, B and C:
$(B + C) \div A = (B \div A) + (C \div A)$ and $(B - C) \div A = (B \div A) - (C \div A)$ [provided A does not equal 0].

◆ These laws are used extensively in multiplication and division calculations.

Further practice

14.1 Use the distributive laws to calculate mentally the cost of 180 textbooks at £8 each, by thinking of the 180 as (a) 100 + 80, (b) 200 – 20.

14.2 Find mentally the total cost of equipping 25 pupils with a textbook costing £12 and a workbook costing £4:

a) using the process represented by A(B +C)

b) using the process represented by AB + AC.

Describe in words the two processes.

14.3 The headteacher of a primary school receives additional funding of £1330 from the PTA for reading books, to be distributed equally across seven year groups. How much is this per year group? Work this out mentally, using the distributive laws of division, by thinking of the £1330 as (a) £700 add something, (b) £1400 subtract something.

Using a four-function calculator, precedence of operators

a) On your calculator enter this calculation just as it is written, reading from left to right: 3 + 4 × 5 =.... Does your calculator give you the 'right' answer?

b) There are 149 pupils from Key Stage 1, 344 pupils from Key Stage 2 and 34 adults, going on a school trip. To calculate how many 68-seater coaches are required, the headteacher enters on a calculator: 149 + 344 + 34 ÷ 68 =... Is this correct?

Answers to check-up 15

a) Your calculator may give the answer 35. Technically this is wrong. The correct answer is 23.

b) If a scientific calculator is used, the answer obtained (494 coaches!) will be incorrect. If a basic four-function calculator is used, the result displayed is 7.75, which means 8 coaches are required. This is correct.

Discussion and explanation of check-up 15

How can a calculator give you the wrong answer? Well, it depends on what kind of a calculator you are using. The problem is that $3 + 4 \times 5$ is ambiguous. Does it mean 3 added to (4×5), or $(3 + 4)$ multiplied by 5? In formal mathematics there is a convention that, unless there are brackets to indicate otherwise, division and multiplication have 'precedence' over addition and subtraction. So, being pedantic, we would have to say that $3 + 4 \times 5$ should mean that you multiply the 4 by the 5 first and then add 3 to this, i.e. $3 + (4 \times 5)$. This convention is especially necessary when manipulating and using algebraic expressions. Normally, in arithmetic calculations the context makes it clear which bits of a mixed calculation should be done first. If there is any possibility of ambiguity it makes sense to put in whatever brackets are necessary. If you mean to do the $3 + 4$ first, write $(3 + 4) \times 5$. If you mean to do the multiplication first, write $3 + (4 \times 5)$.

Now, if your calculator gives you the answer 23 when you enter $3 + 4 \times 5 =$, then you have a scientific calculator that uses what is called an algebraic operating system. In this system, when you ask the calculator to do an addition (like $3 + 4...$) it waits to see if there is a multiplication or division coming next before proceeding. If there is, it does that first! If, however, you get the answer 35, then you have a basic four-function calculator that ignores the mathematician's convention about precedence of operators and just does the operations in the order they are entered. On-screen calculators on personal computers are likely to be of the basic four-function variety. Note also that many of these use an asterisk (*) and a forward slash (/) as symbols for multiplication and division respectively.

So, if the headteacher in (b) enters '149 + 344 + 34 ÷ 68 =' onto a four-function calculator, it will (correctly in this context) add up the first three numbers and then divide by 68. But a scientific calculator would calculate '34 ÷ 68' first before adding it to the sum of 149 and 344. To get a scientific calculator to do the calculation required here, we would have to press the equals key after the 34, to get the addition completed before we do the division by 68.

See also...

Check-up 17: Using the memory on a four-function calculator

Summary of key ideas

◆ There is a convention in formal mathematics that, unless otherwise indicated by brackets, divisions and multiplications in mixed calculations have precedence over additions and subtractions.

◆ In writing down a mixed calculation it is best to use brackets to avoid ambiguity about which parts of the calculation should be done first.

◆ A scientific calculator uses the precedence-of-operators convention.

◆ A basic four-function calculator just does the operations in the order in which they are entered.

Further practice

15.1 What would be displayed if you entered '12 – 6 ÷ 2 =' on (a) a basic four-function calculator, (b) a scientific calculator with an algebraic operating system?

15.2 For the school trip in Check-up 15 question (b), the headteacher wants to check the child–adult ratio and enters on a calculator: 149 + 344 ÷ 34 =. This gives the result 14.5. What kind of calculator is being used?

Check-Up

16

Using a four-function calculator for money calculations

Use a calculator to find:

a) The total cost of equipping a class of 26 pupils with a textbook costing £5.99 and a workbook costing 86p.

b) What is the cost per pupil of materials costing £948 bought for a year group of 123 pupils?

c) How many textbooks costing £8.79 can you purchase from a budget of £650?

Answers to check-up 16

a) £178.10.   b) £7.71.   c) 73.

Discussion and explanation of check-up 16

Here are just a few important, but straightforward, reminders about doing money calculations on a calculator. First, when calculating the total cost of a bill, make sure that all the amounts involved are expressed in the same units. So, in (a) we would change the 86p to £0.86, before entering it onto the calculator. With a basic four-function calculator the key sequence would be: 5.99 + 0.86 × 26 = (see Check-up 15). Second, note that there is a convention when expressing amounts of money in pounds always to give two figures after the point. The calculator does not know this convention, so it displays the result as 178.1. This is not £178 and one penny. We have to interpret it as £178.10, writing in the extra zero to make it clear that we have ten pence.

Third, when you do a division on a calculator it will always display all available figures after the decimal point in the answer. In example (b), entering '948 ÷ 123 =' produces the result 7.707317... It makes sense to give the 'cost per pupil' to the nearest penny, so this answer has to be rounded and interpreted as £7.71. We have rounded up, because we are working to the nearest penny and the next figure after 7.70 indicates that we are nearer to 7.71 than 7.70.

In example (c) we enter '650 ÷ 8.79 =' and obtain the result 73.947667. We actually round this answer down to 73. It is the context that determines this, not the figures after the decimal point. We can only buy whole textbooks, so the answer must be given as a whole number. We can only afford 73 textbooks. We have nearly enough for 74, but not quite: that would actually require a budget of £650.46... though I suppose in practice, if we really needed 74 books we would be able to find the extra 46p somewhere!

Finally, remember to check whether your calculator answer looks reasonable, by doing some mental approximations. It is very easy to press a wrong button or make a slip in entering the data. If, for example, I had by accident forgotten to write the 86p as £0.86 in example (a) and entered '5.99 + 86 × 26 =' onto the calculator, I would have got the answer £2391.74. Is this a reasonable answer for the cost of equipping under 30 pupils with less than £7's worth of materials? Obviously, no! I would expect the answer to be less than £210 (30 × £7) and more than £150 (25 × £6).

See also...

Check-up 19: Rounding answers

Check-up 31: Using approximations to check your answers

Summary of key ideas

◆ When calculating the total cost of a bill, express all the amounts involved in the same units (e.g. all in pound-notation).

◆ The convention for amounts of money in pounds is to give two figures after the point. The calculator does not know this and will display a result such as £5.20 with only one figure after the point (5.2).

◆ Results displayed on a calculator that represent amounts of money may have to be rounded to the nearest penny, if there are more than two figures after the point. But sometimes the context determines whether the result should be rounded up or down.

◆ Use mental approximations to check whether a calculator result is reasonable.

Further practice

16.1 If you need to practise using your calculator, find the total cost of the items in this table. Make an estimate first of the total cost.

Item	pencils	cm-square paper	30-cm rulers	markers	erasers
Cost per pack	£4.15	£2.95	£5.45	£3.00	95p
Number of packs	5	3	3	12	4

16.2 Three pupils (A, B and C) get different answers when using a calculator to find the total cost of providing a drink (37p), a packet of crisps (28p) and a sandwich (£1.29) for all 68 pupils on a trip: A gets £4507.72, B gets £152.72 and C gets £131.92. Without using a calculator, which of these is likely to be correct? Now use a calculator to find the total cost.

16.3 A pupil uses a calculator and finds the cost of 46 calculators at £3.95 each to be 'one hundred and eighty-one pounds, seven pence'. What mistake has been made here?

Check-Up

17

Using the memory on a four-function calculator

Pupils' marks in four pieces of coursework (A, B, C and D) are combined to give an overall mark by using the formula: (3A + 2.5B + 1.5C + 5D)/12. Use a four-function calculator with a memory facility to find the overall mark obtained by a pupil for whom A = 57, B = 69, C = 78 and D = 49. Give the result to one decimal place.

Answers to check-up 17

58.791666667, which is 58.8 rounded to one decimal place.

Discussion and explanation of check-up 17

Putting in lots of brackets to show what must be done first, we have to calculate $[(3 \times 57) + (2.5 \times 69) + (1.5 \times 78) + (5 \times 49)] \div 12$. Using a basic four-function calculator, each of the multiplications here has to be done separately. If the calculator does not have a memory store, then there is nothing for it but to write down the intermediate results and then enter them again to get the total to be divided by 12. But if your basic four-function calculator does have a memory store, the most efficient procedure is to use this and thus to avoid having to write down the intermediate results. A calculator with a memory store will have buttons such as:

MRC: for recalling whatever is currently stored in the memory

M+:   for adding the number on display to what is currently stored in the memory

M– :   for subtracting the number on display from the memory.

On my basic calculator, pressing MRC twice clears the memory. It is obviously good practice always to do this before embarking on a calculation using the memory facility. So, for example, to do the calculation $(3.4 \times 4.8) – (1.2 \times 2.7)$ on such a calculator, I could use this key sequence: MRC, MRC (to clear the memory), $3.4 \times 4.8 =$, M+, $1.2 \times 2.7 =$, M–, MRC. Try this on your calculator. Alternatively, I could enter: MRC, MRC, $1.2 \times 2.7 =$, M+, $3.4 \times 4.8 –$ MRC =. Do this as well and try to follow what is going on.

To perform the complete calculation in Check-up 17, I use this key sequence: MRC, MRC (to clear the memory), $3 \times 57 =$, M+, $2.5 \times 69 =$, M+, $1.5 \times 78 =$, M+, $5 \times 49 =$, M+, MRC, $\div 12 =$.

Most on-screen calculators on computers do not have a memory store, although you can often use the 'copy' facility to save the number currently displayed to enter it again later (or elsewhere).

Incidentally, with a scientific calculator, the whole calculation could be entered in one go, without using the memory facility, as follows: $3 \times 57 + 2.5$

$\times$ 69 + 1.5 $\times$ 78 + 5 $\times$ 49 = $\div$ 12. This works because such a calculator gives precedence to multiplication over addition. Notice that we enter '=' before the final division by 12, to get the calculator to complete the addition before the division.

See also...

Check-up 15: Using a four-function calculator, precedence of operators

Check-up 20: Very large and very small numbers

Summary of key ideas

Using a basic four-function calculator with a memory store:

◆   Remember to clear the memory before starting a new calculation (e.g. by pressing MRC twice).

◆   Use the M+ button to add what is displayed at any stage of the calculation to what is currently in the memory, and the M− button to subtract what is displayed from what is currently in the memory, thus avoiding the need to write down intermediate results.

◆   There will be a button (e.g. MRC) to recall what is currently in the memory.

Further practice

17.1 If your calculator has a memory facility and you did not use it for Further Practice question 16.1, return to this question now and do it again using the MRC and M+ buttons.

17.2 What result would I get if I entered the following key sequence onto my basic four-function calculator: MRC, MRC, 12 ÷ 4 =, M+, 3 × 5 =, M+, 2 × 4 =, M−, MRC?

17.3 The table below shows one year's annual age-weighted allocation of LEA funding to a primary school per pupil, with the number of pupils in the year groups of a particular school. Use a four-function calculator with a memory facility to calculate the total allocation for this school, without writing down any intermediate results.

	Year R	Year 1	Year 2	Year 3	Year 4	Year 5	Year 6
Allocation per pupil	£1328	£1395	£1391	£1376	£1359	£1399	£1402
Number of pupils	45	58	63	59	60	64	53

Check-Up

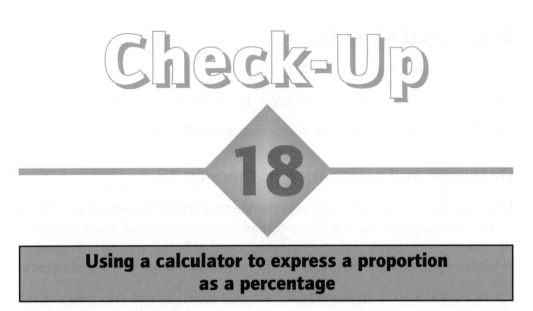

Using a calculator to express a proportion as a percentage

A local education authority survey of the length of the Key Stage 2 taught week (in hours, rounded to one decimal place) in its primary schools produced the data shown in the table below. Fill in the total number of schools involved and then, using a calculator, the percentages of schools in each band, giving these to one decimal place. How many schools are falling short of the recommended 23.5 teaching-hours per week? What percentage of schools is this?

Weekly teaching-hours	20.5–21.4	21.5–22.4	22.5–23.4	23.5–24.4	24.5–25.4	25.5–26.4	26.5–27.4	Total
Number of schools	2	8	63	169	87	11	1	
Percentage of schools								

Answers to check-up 18

The total number of schools is 341.

The percentages are: 0.6%, 2.3%, 18.5%, 49.6%, 25.5%, 3.2%, 0.3%.

73 schools (21.4%) fall short of the recommended 23.5 hours.

Discussion and explanation of check-up 18

In Check-ups 1 and 2 we saw how to change proportions to percentages, using mental and informal methods. The proportions involved in this check-up are too complicated to calculate as percentages mentally, because 341 is not easily related to 100 or any multiples of 100. So it makes sense to use a calculator.

There are 63 schools in the 22.5-23.4 hours band, out of the total of 341 schools. To express this proportion as a decimal, we simply have to calculate $63 \div 341$ (see Check-up 10). My calculator gives me the result 0.18475073314. In Check-up 3 we saw that to change a decimal to an equivalent percentage all we have to do is to move the figures two places to the left. This gives us the proportion of schools in this band as 18.475073314%. Clearly, there are too many figures here and it is suggested that we round the results to one decimal place. Since the figure following the 18.4 is greater than 5, we round *up* to 18.5%. Notice that moving the figures two places to the left is equivalent to multiplying by 100. So, you could enter this key sequence on your calculator: $63 \div 341 \times 100$. You might consider, however, whether getting the calculator to multiply by 100 for you is just a little lazy!

All the other percentages are worked out in the same way. For example, 11 out of 341 is calculated using $11 \div 341 = 0.03225806452 = 3.225806452\% = 3.2\%$ to one decimal place.

Notice particularly that some of the percentages here are less than 1%. The one school in the highest band represents only 0.29325513196% of all the schools, which rounds to 0.3%. This means '0.3 in 100', which is equivalent to '3 in 1000'. This result indicates why it was a good idea to round the percentages to at least one decimal place. If we had been rounding to the nearest whole percent, this would have been recorded as 0%.

See also...

Check-up 3: Decimals and percentages

Check-up 19: Rounding answers

Summary of key ideas

◆   To change a fraction to a percentage, using a calculator:

- divide the numerator by the denominator, to produce a decimal answer

- then move the figures two places to the left in relation to the decimal point (or, to put it another way, multiply by 100)

- and finally, round the answer to an appropriate number of figures.

Further practice

18.1 The following table shows the number of days that five pupils (A, B, C, D, E) were absent out of 190 days. Using a calculator where necessary, fill in the percentage of absences for each pupil, correct to one decimal place.

Pupil...	A	B	C	D	E
Number of days absent	38	23	19	5	1
Percentage of absences					

Check-Up

19

Rounding answers

The table shows the numbers of various A-level grades achieved by female and male candidates in England, Wales and Northern Ireland in one particular year, together with the total number of entries. Using a calculator, express the numbers given for A-grades and B-grades for females as percentages of the number of female entries, and the numbers given for A-grades and B-grades for males as percentages of the number of male entries: (a) to the nearest percent, (b) to one decimal place, (c) to two decimal places. Which of these seems the most appropriate way to give the percentages?

Grades	A	B	C	D	E	N	U	No. of entries
Females	58 364	67 566	75 318	70 680	54 849	31 673	27 811	386 261
Males	57 125	57 469	63 664	61 580	48 178	29 270	26 842	344 128

Answers to check-up 19

a) Females: A-grades 15%, B-grades 17%. Males: A-grades 17%, B-grades 17%.

b) Females: A-grades 15.1%, B-grades 17.5%. Males: A-grades 16.6%, B-grades 16.7%.

c) Females: A-grades 15.11%, B-grades 17.49%. Males: A-grades 16.60%, B-grades 16.70%.

It is probably appropriate to give the results to one decimal place, as in (b).

Discussion and explanation of check-up 19

We often find ourselves in the position of having more figures in the result of a mathematical calculation than we can usefully use. A teacher calculating the result of a 3.5% increase in her salary of £21,565 might get the answer 22319.775 on her calculator, but would probably think of it as 'about £22,300'. In such circumstances we often round answers to the nearest something, such as, in this case, to the nearest hundred pounds. Not always, of course. If I was calculating how many 68-seater buses I needed for 370 pupils and adults going on a school trip (370 ÷ 68 = 5.4411764 on my calculator), then rounding to the nearest whole number (5) would result in having to leave 30 passengers behind! The first important consideration, therefore, is the context that gave rise to the calculation. Especially when handling statistical data, however, it will often be appropriate to round answers to the nearest something, as in the example in this check-up.

My calculator gives the proportion of A-grades for males to be 16.599928%. To round this to the nearest whole percent, we have to choose between 16% and 17%. Halfway between these is 16.5%. The answer is larger than this, so we round up to 17%. To round 16.599928% to one decimal place, we have to choose between 16.5% and 16.6%. Halfway between these is 16.55%. The answer is larger than this, so we round up to 16.6%. To round 16.599928% to two decimal places, we have to choose between 16.59% and 16.60%. Halfway between these is 16.595%. The answer is larger than this, so again we round up, to 16.60%. Notice that it is important to give this answer as 16.60%, not just 16.6%, to indicate that it is correct to two decimal places.

What about rounding the proportion of A-grades for females (15.1099904%)? To the nearest percent we round down to 15%. To one decimal place we round down to 15.1%. Rounding to two decimal places we have to choose between 15.10% and 15.11%. Halfway between these is 15.105%. The answer is larger than this, so we round up to 15.11%.

In deciding how many places to round to, we have to make sure we retain enough information to discriminate between different answers, but not so much that the figures become meaningless.

See also...

Check-up 20: Very large and very small numbers

Summary of key ideas

◆   To round an answer to a given number of decimal places:

- first decide between which two values with that number of decimal places the answer lies (e.g. 5.6481 lies between 5.64 and 5.65, to two decimal places)

- then note what comes halfway between these two values (e.g. 5.645)

- if your answer is greater than this, round up; if it is less, round down (5.6481 is greater than 5.645, so round up to 5.65).

◆   Always consider the context that gave rise to the calculation before rounding the answer.

◆   Give enough figures in the rounded results to be able to discriminate effectively between the data; but not so many that the data is difficult to take in and evaluate at a glance.

Further practice

19.1 Using a calculator, express the proportions of C-grades, D-grades, E-grades and N-grades in the table in Check-up 19 as percentages, rounding them to one decimal place.

19.2 Why would it not be appropriate to give these proportions to the nearest whole percent? For example, look at the male and female results for D-grades and those for N-grades.

Check-Up

20

Very large and very small numbers

a) A teacher's personal computer has 8 Gb (gigabytes) of memory available. Which of the following would be alternative ways of expressing this:

A eight thousand million bytes

B 8 000 000 000 bytes

C 8×10^9 bytes

D 8E9

b) A total of 8 pupils gained no marks in a sample of 2207 of those who took the Key Stage 2 handwriting test. To express this proportion as a decimal, I entered 8/2207 onto my on-screen calculator. The answer displayed was 3.6248301E−3. What does this mean? What percentage of the sample gained no marks?

Answers to check-up 20

a) A, B, C and D are all different ways of expressing 8 gigabytes.

b) It means 3.6248301×10^{-3}, which equals 0.0036248301. That's about 0.4%.

Discussion and explanation of check-up 20

The prefix *giga* means 'a thousand million', what is called a billion in the USA, and nowadays in most other countries as well. Other prefixes sometimes used for large numbers include kilo (k) for a thousand, and mega (M) for a million. So, 8 gigabytes is 8 000 000 000 bytes. Notice that I have used the convention of separating the digits into groups of 3 by using spaces. Sometimes you will see commas used for this purpose (i.e. 8,000,000,000), but this can be confusing because some countries use the comma for a decimal point.

Because it is difficult to take in the size of numbers like this at a glance, you will sometimes see them expressed in what is called *scientific notation*. To do this, we first move the decimal point so that it sits to the right of the first digit in the number. In this case, we get 8.000000000, which is actually just 8. Then you indicate with a *power* of 10, how many times you have to multiply this by 10 to get the original number. Because we have to multiply the 8 by 10 a total of nine times to get back to 8 000 000 000, we can write this big number as 8×10^9. This is shorthand for $8 \times 10 \times 10 \times 10 \times 10 \times 10 \times 10 \times 10 \times 10 \times 10$. Basic four-function calculators will usually just give up when the numbers get too large to display. But some calculators will use a version of scientific notation, for example, writing our number as 8E9. The E stands for 'exponent', a word that is synonymous with 'power of 10'. So, for example, we could write 123 400 000 000 as 1.234×10^{11}, but on some calculators this will be displayed as 1.234E11.

This scientific notation also works for very small numbers, but now a negative exponent is used to indicate how many times you have to *divide* by 10. So, for example, the answer to $8 \div 2207$ will be displayed on many calculators as 0.0036248. In scientific notation this is 3.6248×10^{-3}. The decimal point has been moved to the right of the first non-zero digit. This 3.6248×10^{-3} is therefore shorthand for $3.6248 \div 10 \div 10 \div 10$. Again, we note that some calculators will display this using an E to indicate the exponent, like this: 3.6248E–3. This is what my on-screen calculator does, but it is also able to give more figures after the decimal point (not that I want them).

Scientific notation is useful because the power of 10 is much more significant in indicating the size of number we are dealing with than the actual digits involved.

See also...

Check-up 19: Rounding answers

Summary of key ideas

◆　　To write a large number in scientific notation, move the decimal point to the right of the leading digit and then indicate with a power of 10 how many times this has to be multiplied by 10 (e.g. $650\,000 = 6.5 \times 10 \times 10 \times 10 \times 10 \times 10 = 6.5 \times 10^5$).

◆　　To write a very small number in scientific notation, move the decimal point to the right of the first non-zero digit and then indicate with a negative power of 10 how many times this has to be divided by 10 (e.g. $0.00065 = 6.5 \div 10 \div 10 \div 10 \div 10 = 6.5 \times 10^{-4}$).

◆　　Some calculators use a version of scientific notation, where an E followed by a number is used to indicate the power (exponent) of ten (e.g. 6.5E5 and 6.5E–4).

Further practice

20.1 Arrange these approximate populations (data for 1996) in numerical order from smallest to largest:

India: 9.4×10^8 Japan: 1.3×10^8 UK: 5.8×10^7 China 1.2×10^9

20.2 The DfES proposes to provide £290 million pounds for school improvement in England. Write this amount out in full, and in scientific notation.

20.3 In the previous year to that in Check-up 20 question (b), a total of 9 pupils gained no marks in a sample of 2008 of those who took the Key Stage 2 handwriting test. To express this proportion as a decimal, I entered 9/2008 onto my on-screen calculator. The answer displayed was 4.4820717E–3. What does this mean? What percentage of the sample is this?

Check-Up

21

Mental calculations, multiplication strategies

The QCA report on the 1998 Key Stage 3 mathematics National Curriculum assessment expressed concern about the fact that most pupils attempted the calculations below by using a standard multiplication written method. Very few responses indicated that pupils had used appropriate mental or informal strategies. How could they have done this?

a) 46×8

b) Audio cassettes cost £1.49 each. What is the cost of 4 cassettes?

Answers to check-up 21

The answers are (a) 368, and (b) £5.96. Possible methods are discussed below.

Discussion and explanation of check-up 21

When you are presented with a calculation, automatically turning to a standard procedure (like long multiplication) is an indication of a lack of confidence with number. Try to build up a range of informal strategies that you can use. These will be a combination of mental methods and informal written notes. Which strategies you use will depend on the actual numbers involved.

For example, many people find 'doubling' to be the easiest multiplication. So 46×8 could be tackled by doubling 46 (to get $46 \times 2 = 92$), doubling again (to get $46 \times 4 = 184$) and doubling again (to get $46 \times 8 = 368$). In fact, any multiplication with whole numbers can be done by using just doubling. For example, to find 27×19, using repeated doubling we could jot down:

$$27 \times 1 = 27 \quad 27 \times 2 = 54 \quad 27 \times 4 = 108 \quad 27 \times 8 = 216 \quad 27 \times 16 = 432$$

Now, since $19 = 16 + 2 + 1$ for 27×19 we just add 432, 54 and 27, to get the answer, 513.

What we are doing here is to distribute the multiplication by 27 across the addition of 16, 2 and 1:

$$27 \times (16 + 2 + 1) = (27 \times 16) + (27 \times 2) + (27 \times 1)$$

An easier way of using the distributive law here would be to think of the 19 as $(20 - 1)$:

$$27 \times 19 = 27 \times (20 - 1) = (27 \times 20) - (27 \times 1) = 540 - 27 = 513$$

This is also how you might have done 46×8 and $4 \times £1.49$:

$$46 \times 8 = (40 + 5 + 1) \times 8 = (40 \times 8) + (5 \times 8) + (1 \times 8) = 320 + 40 + 8 = 368$$

$$4 \times £1.49 = 4 \times (£1.50 - £0.01) = (4 \times £1.50) - (4 \times £0.01) =$$
$$£6.00 - £0.04 = £5.96$$

Of course, there's no need to write out all these steps in full like this. Just jot down what you need to remember to keep track of where you are in the mental calculation. The trick is to look for related calculations that are easier to do mentally. You can do this by subtraction (like changing the £1.49 to £1.50 – £0.01) or by addition (like changing 46 into 40 + 5 + 1), or a mixture of the two. You can also do it by spotting useful *factors*. For example, whenever I see 25 in a multiplication I want to multiply it by 4! So, if I had to calculate 25 × 36, I would split the 36 into its factors (4 × 9) and change 25 × 36 to 25 × 4 × 9, which is then just 100 × 9 = 900.

See also...

Check-up 12: The commutative laws

Check-up 13: The associative laws

Check-up 14: The distributive laws

Check-up 22: Mental calculations, division strategies

Summary of key ideas

◆ Many multiplications can be done by a combination of mental calculations and a few jottings to keep track of where you are.

◆ One strategy is to use doubling and to build up the number by which you are multiplying using a combination of 1, 2, 4, 8, 16 and so on.

◆ Look for easier, related multiplications, by changing one of the numbers into a sum of easier numbers (e.g. 28 = 25 + 2 + 1) or a difference (e.g. 28 = 30 – 2), and then using the distributive law.

◆ Try splitting up one of the numbers into factors that might make the multiplication easier.

Further practice

Use a range of informal strategies, combining mental calculations with whatever jottings are needed, to answer the following questions. These are the level
of multiplication calculations that you should be able to do without using a
calculator and without resorting to 'long multiplication'! The methods given
in the answers are just some of many possibilities for appropriate strategies.

21.1 Find the cost of 24 computer discs at £4.95 each.

21.2 A primary school with 125 pupils is eligible for an additional grant of
£48 per pupil for numeracy support. How much is this in total?

21.3 A pupil's text has about 240 words per page: approximately how many
words in a text of 97 pages?

21.4 A school playing field is planned to be 45 metres long and 74 metres wide.
What is the total area, in square metres? (Multiply the length by the
width.) Would a field of 44 m by 75 m be larger, smaller or the same area?

Check-Up

22

Mental calculations, division strategies

Without resorting to a formal method like long division or a calculator, use a combination of mental calculations and informal jottings to find the number of pupils per teacher for each of these schools:

a)   School A: 252 pupils, 12 teachers

b)   School B: 805 pupils, 35 teachers

c)   School C: 785 pupils, 44 teachers

Answers to check-up 22

a) 21.   b) 23.   c) nearly 18.

Possible methods are discussed below.

Discussion and explanation of check-up 22

We should be able to handle divisions of this level of difficulty without recourse to a calculator or formal written methods, such as long division. Informal methods are usually much easier than long division anyway. The calculations in this check-up illustrate some useful strategies.

For $252 \div 12$, I might use the fact that you do not change the value of the ratio if you divide both numbers by the same thing. This is exactly the same as the process of 'cancelling' in fractions (see Check-up 10). In this example, I could easily halve each number to change the calculation to $126 \div 6$. Halve them again: $63 \div 3$. Then complete the calculation, thinking of the 63 as $60 + 3$: $63 \div 3 = (60 \div 3) + (3 \div 3) = 20 + 1 = 21$. This last step is using the distributive law (see Check-up 14).

You also do not change the value of a ratio if you multiply both numbers by the same thing. This is particularly useful when the number you are dividing by ends in a 5. For example, for $805 \div 35$, I would double both numbers, to get $1610 \div 70$. Then divide both by 10: $161 \div 7$. Think of the 161 as $140 + 21$: $161 \div 7 = (140 \div 7) + (21 \div 7) = 20 + 3$.

Why did I think of changing 161 to $140 + 21$? Because I am always on the lookout for numbers that divide easily. If I have to divide by 7 then the number closest to 161 that looks friendly is 140.

So, given $785 \div 44$, I would think: I wish it was $880 \div 44$, because that would just be 20. But that would be using 95 too many pupils. Now I think: I wish that 95 was 88, because $88 \div 44 = 2$. But that would be using 7 too many pupils. So if there were just 7 more pupils, the ratio would be $20 - 2 = 18$. The total of 7 pupils we are missing to give us the pupil–teacher ratio of 18 is less than half a pupil for each one of the 44 teachers, so clearly the PTR rounded to the nearest whole number is 18. If you need the result to be more precise than this then you should probably use a calculator.

In other contexts, the answer to $785 \div 44$ might have been 17. For example, how many graphic calculators costing £44 each can you buy with £785? In this case you are £7 short of what you need for 18 calculators, so you can actually only afford 17, leaving you with £35 left to spend.

See also...

Check-up 10: Fractions to decimals and vice versa

Check-up 14: The distributive laws

Check-up 37: Simplifying ratios

Summary of key ideas

◆　It is usually easier to do a division by a one- or two-digit number using informal methods than using a formal process like long division.

◆　One way of simplifying a division calculation is to multiply or divide both numbers involved by the same thing (e.g. change 225 ÷ 15 to 450 ÷ 30, by doubling; change 450 ÷ 30 to 45 ÷ 3 by dividing by 10).

◆　Another strategy is to look for easier, related divisions, by relating the number you are dividing to a combination of numbers that are easier to divide, using addition and subtraction (e.g. for 198 ÷ 9 change the 198 to 180 + 18; for 198 ÷ 22 change the 198 to 220 − 22).

Further practice

The questions here illustrate the level of division calculations you should be able to manage without a calculator, using informal jottings and mental calculations. The answers provide just some suggestions for how to tackle these – you may have better methods.

22.1 The QCA report on the 1998 Key Stage 3 mathematics National Curriculum assessments comments that most pupils attempted to calculate 144 ÷ 9 by using a formal written division method. How else might they have done it more easily?

22.2 A small primary school with 85 pupils spends £6035 on learning resources one year. How much is this per pupil?

22.3 To find the average mark achieved by pupils in an English test, the teacher adds up all the marks (total 893) and divides by the number of pupils (24). What is the result to the nearest whole number?

Check-Up

23

Mental calculations, finding a percentage of a quantity

You should be able to handle questions such as the following, mentally, without the use of a calculator or any formal procedures.

a) What is 40% of 55?

b) A total of 83% of 600 schools participate in an LEA appointments pool. How many schools do not participate?

c) VAT at 17.5% is to be added to the price of £240 for a TV set. How much VAT is payable?

d) A school's target for their Key Stage 3 pupils is that 65% of them should achieve at least level 5 in the English national assessment. If one year they have 180 pupils entering, how many must reach level 5 to achieve the target?

Answers to check-up 23

a) 22.   b) 102.   c) £42.   d) 117 pupils.

Discussion and explanation of check-up 23

Since 40% = $\frac{2}{5}$ and we can find a fifth of 55 very easily (11), the simplest approach with (a) is to think of the 40% as the equivalent fraction (two-fifths), so 40% of 55 is 22.

Otherwise, to handle percentage calculations mentally, start from what you know, or can work out easily, and then work your way gradually to the required percentage. A good starting point is often 10%, which, because it's equal to a tenth, is usually very simple to find. For example, in (b), because 83% participate and so 17% do not (100% − 83% = 17%), we need to work out 17% of 600. Now 17% can be made up from 10%, 5%, 1% and 1%, all of which I can jot down instantly: 10% of 600 is 60; 5% is half of that, 30; 1% of 600 is just 6 (1 per 100). So 17% of 600 = 60 + 30 + 6 + 6 = 102. To find the VAT in (c) I would again start with 10%, then halve this to get 5%, and halve this to get 2.5%. Adding these will give 17.5%: £24 + £12 + £6 = £42. In (d) we need 65% of 180. Here I would make up the 65% from 50%, 10% and 5%: 90 + 18 + 9 = 117.

This *ad hoc* method is surprisingly efficient, even with percentage calculations that look unpromising. You can also involve subtraction if it helps. For example, to find 74% of 294 you do not really need a calculator, because you can work around 75%:

50% of 294	=	147	(half of 294)
25% of 294	=	73.5	(half of the 50%)
75% of 294	=	220.5	(adding the 50% and 25%, 147.0 + 73.5)
1% of 294	=	2.94	(one hundredth)
74% of 294	=	217.56	(75% − 1%, i.e. 220.50 − 2.94)

Notice that to find 1% of a number you have to divide by 100. This results in all the figures moving two places to the right in relation to the decimal point. Notice also, when calculating a sum or difference involving decimals, it is safest to put in extra zeros to ensure that the numbers have the same number of figures after the decimal point (e.g. 147.0 + 73.5, 220.50 – 2.94).

See also...

Check-up 24: Finding a percentage of a quantity using a calculator

Check-up 25: Adding and subtracting decimals

Summary of key ideas

◆ To find a percentage of a quantity, if the percentage required is equivalent to a simple fraction (like 75% = $\frac{3}{4}$, 40% = $\frac{2}{5}$) that can be worked out easily, then use that fraction.

◆ Otherwise, for mental and informal calculations of percentages of a quantity, build up the required percentage from percentages that are easy to calculate, such as 10%, 5%, 1%, 2%, 50%, 25%).

Further practice

Do these questions without using a calculator, by mental and informal, *ad hoc* methods.

23.1 What is (a) 12.5% of 160? (b) 30% of 220?

23.2 A secondary school's target for English GCSE results is that at least 78% of its pupils should achieve grade C or above. How many pupils is that out of a cohort of 240?

23.3 In a year group of 125 pupils, 40% achieved level 5 or above in the Key Stage 2 English test and 36% achieved level 4. How many pupils did not reach level 4?

Check-Up

24

Finding a percentage of a quantity using a calculator

a) One question in a Key Stage 2 reading assessment asks pupils to identify the main contrasts that a poet makes in two parts of a poem. This proves to be challenging, with the QCA reporting that 61.98% pupils out of a sample of 2207 score zero out of a possible three marks for this question. How many pupils is this?

b) In 1998, out of 1508 requests for review of the marking of the work of individual pupils in the Key Stage 3 English national tests, 63.26% resulted in a change of level. How many was this?

Answer to check-up 24

a) 1368.   b) 954.

Discussion and explanation of check-up 24

For the calculation of percentages as complicated as those in this check-up, clearly the use of a calculator is justified and appropriate.

There are three procedures for using a basic calculator to find a percentage of a quantity. For example, consider finding 79% of 186.

First you can use the fact that 79% means $\frac{79}{100}$. So, we have to find 100th of 186 (i.e. divide it by 100) and then multiply this by 79. The key sequence would be: 186 ÷ 100 × 79 =. This gives the result 146.94, which we may or may not want to round, depending on the context. Actually, you can enter the multiplication and the division here in any order. For example, you could enter '186 × 79 ÷ 100 =', or '79 × 186 ÷ 100 =', or '79 ÷ 100 × 186'. Try them all and confirm that the answers are the same.

Secondly, you might have a percent key (%) on your calculator. These can be quite idiosyncratic, so you will need to find out how yours works. On one of my calculators I would enter '79, %, ×, 186, =' and get the right result. On my more basic calculator this would not work; I would have to enter '186, ×, 79, %'.

On-screen calculators often do not have a percent key. So in this case you may choose to use the first procedure given above. But the third procedure I have to offer seems to me the simplest and quickest. Remember that a percentage can very easily be converted to a decimal number, just by moving the figures two places to the right in relation to the decimal point. So 79% becomes 0.79. This means I can find 79% of 186 just by calculating 0.79 × 186.

So, in (a) we have to find 61.98% of 2207. I would just use my calculator to find 0.6198 × 2207, which gives 1367.8986, which, to the nearest whole number, is 1368 pupils. Alternatively, you could enter, say, '61.98 × 2207 ÷ 100 =', or use the percent key if you have one.

Similarly, in (b) we have to find 63.26% of 1508. My calculator gives me 0.6326 × 1508 = 953.9608, which, to the nearest whole number, is 954 reviews. Alternatively, you could enter, say, '1508 ÷ 100 × 63.26 =', or use the percent key if you have one.

See also...

Check-up 9: Finding a fraction of a quantity

Check-up 39: Increasing or decreasing by a percentage

Summary of key ideas

◆　　There are three procedures for using a calculator to find a percentage of a number (e.g. to find 37% of 89).

◆　　First, you can multiply by the percentage and divide by 100 (e.g. 89 × 37 ÷ 100 =).

◆　　Second you can use the percent key, if you have one (e.g. 89 × 37%), but you need to find out how your calculator does this.

◆　　Third, change the percentage mentally to a decimal (e.g. 0.37 × 89 =).

Further practice

24.1 Nationally, 47.8% of Year 11 pupils achieved five or more grades A*–C in the GCSE examinations, in one particular year. A school with 279 pupils in Year 10 aims to surpass that in the following year's examinations. How many of these pupils must achieve five or more grades A*–C? Answer this using all three of the calculator methods explained in this check-up.

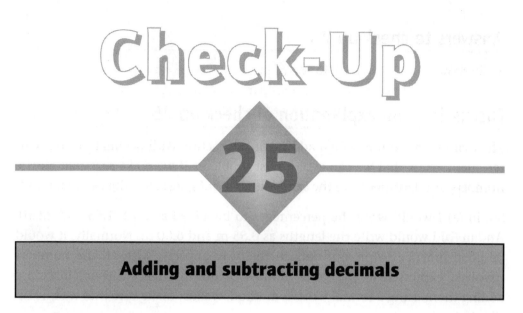

Check-Up

25

Adding and subtracting decimals

Do not use a calculator.

a) Of the Key Stage 1 pupils who entered the special mathematics assessment at level 4 and above in the national tests in 1998, 2.12% achieved level 6, 1.63% achieved level 5 and 22.1% achieved level 4. Add these to find the total percentage of these pupils that achieved at least level 4.

b) If 0.55 m is cut off a tape of length 6 m, what length remains?

Answers to check-up 25

a) 25.85%.   b) 5.45 m.

Discussion and explanation of check-up 25

The main thing to note when adding or subtracting with decimals, using written methods, is that we can avoid most problems if we make sure that all the numbers or quantities have the same number of figures after the decimal point.

So, in (a) I would write the percentages to be added as 2.12, 1.63 and 22.10. And in (b) I would write the lengths as 0.55 m and 6.00 m. Normally, it would be good practice to present data in this way anyway, with all the numbers involved expressed to the same number of decimal places. Then, if we are adding them using a formal written method, we just make sure that we line up the decimal points:

$$
\begin{array}{r}
2.12 \\
1.63 \\
+\ 22.10 \\
\hline
25.85
\end{array}
\qquad
\begin{array}{r}
6.00 \\
-\ 0.55 \\
\hline
5.45
\end{array}
$$

You should really be able to do the calculation of 6 – 0.55 mentally. The diagram below uses what is sometimes called an 'empty number-line'. This does not have a scale on it and so the sizes of the gaps between the numbers are not to scale. The diagram provides a powerful mental image. The 0.55 has been removed and we have to find the size of the gap from 0.55 to 6. We can do this using 0.6 and 1 as 'stepping-stones', giving three bits to add: 5 + 0.4 + 0.05, which equals 5.45.

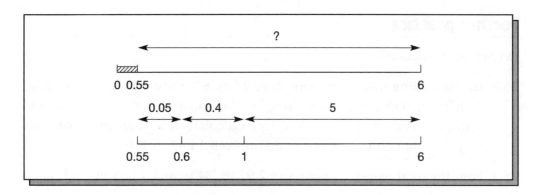

See also...

Check-up 3: Decimals and percentages

Check-up 33: Knowledge of metric units of length and distance

---

Summary of key ideas

◆   For written calculations involving addition or subtraction with decimals, write each number or quantity with the same number of figures after the decimal point.

◆   Then for formal calculations in a vertical format, ensure that the decimal points are lined up.

◆   To find differences between decimal numbers (e.g. 3.1 – 1.42) informally, use an empty number-line with appropriate numbers as stepping-stones (e.g. 1.42... 1.5... 2... 3... 3.1).

Further practice

Do not use a calculator.

25.1 In the spelling test for the Key Stage 2 English assessment one year, only 14.87% of pupils were able to spell 'particularly' correctly. What percentage failed to spell it correctly? Calculate this mentally, using an empty number-line picture to add on from 14.87 to 100.

25.2 Find the total length in metres of 2.97 m, 34 m and 1.085 m.

25.3 Find the difference between 3.62 m and 2.085 m.

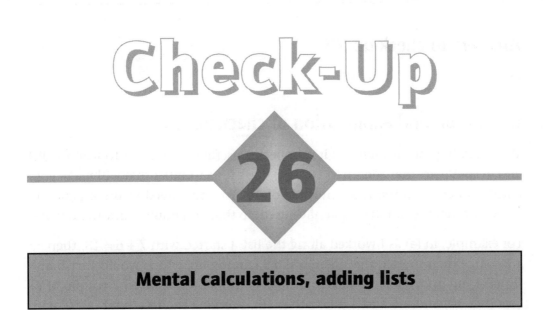

Check-Up

26

Mental calculations, adding lists

You should be able mentally and speedily to add lists of numbers such as those in this check-up, without recourse to a calculator or a formal written method.

a) A pupil's marks out of 10 in ten weekly tests are: 7, 6, 8, 5, 9, 6, 5, 4, 3, 6. What is the pupil's total mark out of 100?

b) The numbers of pupils in the classes of a primary school are 18, 25, 26, 29, 31, 28 and 27. How many pupils altogether in the school?

Answers to check-up 26

a) 59.   b) 184.

Discussion and explanation of check-up 26

When adding lists of single-digit numbers, a useful technique is to scan the list and to spot pairs that add up to 10. Also, look for a number that will make your current total up to the next multiple of 10. You may need to use a pencil to score through the numbers you have used, so that you don't count them twice.

For example, in (a) as I worked along the list, I started with 7 + 6 = 13, then 13 + 8 = 21. I then spotted that there was a 9 coming up, which would very hand-ily take me up to 30, the next multiple of 10. I then spotted a couple of 5s (another 10) and a 6 and a 4 (another 10), bringing me to a total of 50, with just the final 3 and 6 to add on. Teachers often have to add strings of numbers like these. The numerate teacher will not need a calculator for this task, but will race through the addition at high speed. If that does not describe you yet, then note the techniques recommended here and practise!

When it comes to adding strings of two-digit numbers mentally, in contrast to formal written methods, most of us prefer to handle the tens first. Then, extending the strategies above, we will particularly be on the look-out for any pairs that add to a multiple of 10. For example, in (b) your eye might imme-diately light upon the 29 and the 31, which conveniently sum to 60. I found myself starting from here, then adding on the tens from the remaining class-es, for some reason working from right to left: 60 + 20 = 80, 80 + 20 = 100, 100 + 20 = 120, 120 + 20 = 140, 140 + 10 = 150. I jotted this down. I was then left with the remaining units: 8, 5, 6, 8, 7. The 8 and 5 give 13, to which I added the 7 to get to 20. Then, adding on 6 and 8 (14) gave 34, which added to the 150 gave me 184 for the total.

Another mental technique is to add a number like 29 by adding 30 and then sub-tracting 1. Similarly, to add 28 you could add 30 and subtract 2. This process is sometimes called compensation: add a bit more than you need, then compensate.

Even if you do decide to write the string of numbers to be added in a vertical column with the hundreds, tens and units lined up, you should still use the techniques suggested for adding strings of single-digit numbers for getting the totals in each column.

See also...

Check-up 25: Adding and subtracting decimals

Summary of key ideas

◆　　When adding lists of single-digit numbers, scan the list and spot pairs that add up to 10.

◆　　Also look for a number that will make your current total up to the next multiple of 10.

◆　　Most people start with the tens digits when adding a string of two-digit numbers mentally.

◆　　Look for pairs of numbers that make up a multiple of 10 (e.g. 43 and 17).

◆　　To add a number close to a multiple of 10 (e.g. 48 is nearly 50), you can add the multiple of 10 and then compensate (e.g. add 50 and subtract 2).

Further practice

All you really need to do for further practice is to write out strings of one- and two-digit numbers and practise adding them accurately and speedily! I'll give you two examples to try. Allow yourself 30 seconds for each!

26.1 The numbers of unauthorised absences in a secondary school each day one month were:

9, 2, 5, 6, 12, 6, 7, 8, 1, 12, 9, 4, 5, 6, 9, 1, 2, 0, 8, 15, 3, 2.

What was the monthly total?

26.2 Add up the following marks achieved by a pupil in a series of mathematics tests:

43, 23, 27, 34, 49, 22, 21, 40, 36, 35.

Check-Up

27

More multiplication strategies

A headteacher is calculating the total cost of 47 days' supply cover for a term on the basis of £128 per day. Without using a calculator, what does this come to?

Answer to check-up 27

£6016.

Discussion and explanation of check-up 27

Sometimes you will find yourself in the position of having to do a multiplication calculation like this without a calculator available. Even though the numbers are quite large, you should still be able to tackle it using the informal methods given in Check-up 21. However, you may appreciate having available a formal written method. You may be familiar with the method known as long multiplication. This is shown below on the left. The procedure here first multiplies 128 by 40, then multiplies 128 by 7, and then adds the results. The problem is that calculations like 128 by 40 and 128 by 7 are quite tricky to handle mentally when you are in the middle of a longer calculation.

$$
\begin{array}{rrrr}
 & 1 & 2 & 8 \\
\times & & 4 & 7 \\
\hline
5 & 1 & 2 & 0 \\
 & 8 & 9 & 6 \\
\hline
6 & 0 & 1 & 6 \\
\hline
\end{array}
$$

$\leftarrow$ this is 128×40
$\leftarrow$ this is 128×7

$$
\begin{array}{rcr}
100 \times 40 & = & 4000 \\
100 \times 7 & = & 700 \\
20 \times 40 & = & 800 \\
20 \times 7 & = & 140 \\
8 \times 40 & = & 320 \\
8 \times 7 & = & 56 \\
\hline
 & & 6016 \\
\hline
\end{array}
$$

An alternative, simpler procedure is shown on the right. In this method we partition the 128 into $100 + 20 + 8$ as well as the 47 into $40 + 7$. This then gives us, in this example, six separate multiplications to do, but they are all very easy! The diagram below (not drawn to scale) is a useful picture of what is going on here: each one of the six multiplications involved in finding 128×47 is represented by one of the six areas in the rectangle.

	100	20	8	
	100×40	20×40	8×40	40
	100×7	20×7	8×7	7

If you were multiplying two two-digit numbers, there would be only four areas involved (e.g. for 47×59 you would need 40×50, 40×9, 7×50 and 7×9). With two three-digit numbers, there would be nine areas involved. Any more than this and you really should find the calculator.

See also...

Check-up 21: Mental calculations, multiplication strategies

Summary of key ideas

◆ When a written method is needed for a multiplication calculation, an alternative to long multiplication is to partition each number into hundreds, tens and units and multiply each part of one number by each part of the other, and add all the results.

◆ This procedure can be represented as finding areas of parts of a rectangle, produced by dividing up the sides into hundreds, tens and units.

Further practice

Try using the 'areas' method to find the answers to these questions.

27.1 A school secretary is contracted to work 28 hours per week for 39 weeks of the year. How many hours is this in total?

27.2 The school sports field is a rectangle, 142 metres long and 72 metres wide. Is this more or less than 1 hectare in area? (1 hectare = 10 000 square metres)

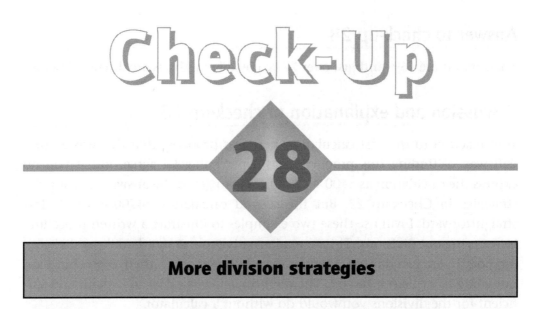

Check-Up

28

More division strategies

In a primary school, a total of 54 out of 72 pupils achieved level 4 or above in the Key Stage 2 science test one year. The following year it was 47 out of 61 pupils. To express these as percentages, a headteacher decides to calculate 5400 ÷ 72 and 4700 ÷ 61. Without a calculator, complete these calculations.

Answer to check-up 28

The answers are 75% and just over 77%. Possible methods are discussed below.

Discussion and explanation of check-up 28

Your reaction to the first calculation here was probably that this was a fairly daft way of finding this proportion as a percentage! I agree. But if you do express the calculation as 5400 ÷ 72, it is easy to get to the answer 75 using the strategies in Check-up 22. But the second calculation (4700 ÷ 61) is less straightforward. I will use these two examples to illustrate a written procedure for carrying out divisions. This is an alternative to the standard 'long division' method. If you can do that, then good luck! If you can't, then, sorry, but I am not going to explain it to you. The method below is easier to explain and sufficient for the divisions you would do without a calculator.

The basis of the method is that we interpret, say, '5400 ÷ 72' as 'how many 72s in 5400?'. We then subtract from the 5400 *ad hoc* lots of 72, using whatever numbers we can handle confidently. When completed, the two calculations here, written out tidily, might look like this:

	5400 ÷ 72			4700 ÷ 61
50	3600		50	3050
	1800			1650
10	720		20	1220
	1080			430
10	720		5	305
	360			125
5	360		2	122
75	0		77	3 rem

In the first example, I started by subtracting 50 lots of 72 from the 5400, because I found that easy to work out (half of 7200, i.e. 3600). I then had 1800 left, so I decided to subtract 10 lots of 72 (720). This left me with 1080, so I could subtract another 10 lots of 72. At this stage I had 360 left and I recognised this as 5 lots of 72. Once these had gone, there was nothing left. Adding up the numbers down the left-hand column gives the total number of 72s in 5400, namely 75.

In the second example, 4700 ÷ 61, I subtracted first 50 lots of 61, then 20 lots, then 5 lots, and, finally, 2 lots of 61. This gives a total of 77 lots of 61, with a remainder of 3. Since this is much less than half of the 61 we are dividing by, the answer is 77 to the nearest whole number.

Take away from the *dividend* (i.e. the number you are dividing) whatever chunks you wish. Your choices will depend on your confidence with mentally multiplying numbers like 61 (the *divisor*). If all you can manage is to multiply by 10, 2 and 1, then that's fine. You'll get there in the end! For example, you could do 4700 ÷ 61 by subtracting 10 lots of 61 (610) repeatedly, seven times in all, leaving you with 430. Then subtract 2 lots of 61 (122), three times, leaving 64. Finally, subtract 1 more 61, to get the result 10 + 10 + 10 + 10 + 10 + 10 + 10 + 2 + 2 + 2 + 1 = 77, with remainder 3.

See also...

Check-up 22: Mental calculations, division strategies

Summary of key ideas

◆   In a division, the number you are dividing is called the dividend; the number you are dividing by is called the divisor (e.g., in 682 ÷ 31, the dividend is 682, the divisor is 31).

◆   A written method for doing divisions, which is an alternative to 'long division', involves interpreting a division statement like '682 ÷ 31' as 'how many 31s are there in 682?'

◆   Answer this by subtracting *ad hoc* lots of the divisor from the dividend, using whatever multiplications you can handle mentally (e.g. from 682, subtract 20 lots of 31, then 2 lots of 31).

◆   The method also works when there is a remainder.

Further practice

28.1 Use the *ad hoc* subtraction method suggested in this check-up to find how many classes of 28 pupils would be needed for a school of 644 pupils.

28.2 Use the *ad hoc* subtraction method to find how many 42-seater coaches would be needed to transport a school party of 1550.

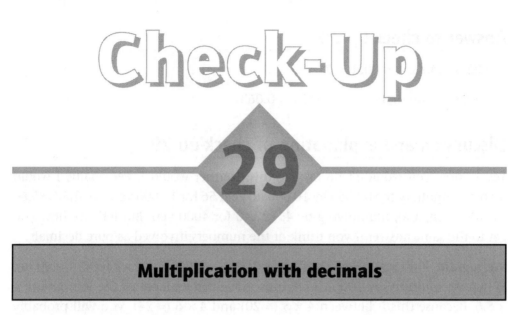

Check-Up

29

Multiplication with decimals

Do not use a calculator.

a) The rate for exchanging Japanese currency to British is 0.0056 pounds sterling per yen. Multiply 0.0056 by 4000 to find the equivalent in British pounds of 4000 Japanese yen.

b) A sheet of A4 paper is approximately 0.3 metres long and 0.21 metres wide. Multiply the length by the width to find the area in square metres.

Answer to check-up 29

a) £22.40 (4000 × 0.0056 = 22.4).

b) 0.063 square metres (0.3 × 0.21 = 0.063).

Discussion and explanation of check-up 29

Yes, I know you wouldn't do (a) like this. Neither would I. Personally, I would mentally multiply the 0.0056 by 10 000, to get £56 for 10 000 yen. So, that's £5.60 for 1000 yen, and, multiplying by 4, £22.40 for 4000 yen. But let's see how you get to the same answer if you think of the numbers involved as pure decimals.

We require 4000 × 0.0056. That's (4 × 1000) × 0.0056 = 4 × (1000 × 0.0056). When we multiply by 1000 the figures move three places to the left, giving 4 × 5.6. Because this is between 4 × 5 (= 20) and 4 × 6 (= 24), you will probably be fairly confident that the answer to this multiplication is 22.4, rather than 2.24 or 224. So, when multiplying by decimals we can often just use our sense of how large the result should be to decide where the decimal point goes in the answer.

But when you come to 0.3 × 0.21, you may be unsure as to whether the answer should be 0.63, 0.063 or even 0.0063. The simplest way of multiplying decimals like this is to change each number into a whole number, by multiplying by 10 as many times as necessary, do the multiplication, and then divide by 10 as many times as you previously multiplied by 10. I'll explain…

0.3 → 3, by multiplying by 10

0.21 → 21, by multiplying by 10 and multiplying by 10 again

Altogether we have multiplied by 10 three times

Then 3 × 21 = 63, but this answer must now be divided by 10 three times → 0.063

Remember that dividing by 10 moves the figures one place to the right.

In practice, you can carry out this procedure by counting how many figures there are altogether after the decimal point in the numbers being multiplied, and then put the decimal point in the place that produces the same number of figures after the point in the answer. For example, for 0.05 × 0.013, we note

that there are five figures in total after the decimal points. Then calculate 5 ×
13 = 65 and just put the decimal point where it gives five figures after the point
in the answer, putting in zeros where necessary: 0.00065.

See also...

Check-up 3: Decimals and percentages

Check-up 30: Division with decimals

Summary of key ideas

◆   Multiplying by 10, 100 or 1000 moves the figures one, two or three
     places respectively to the left in relation to the decimal point.

◆   Dividing by 10, 100 or 1000 moves the figures one, two or three
     places respectively to the right in relation to the decimal point.

◆   To multiply numbers involving decimals (e.g. 0.04 × 1.2)

     –   get rid of the decimal points by multiplying each number by 10
         as many times as necessary (0.04 → 4, 1.2 → 12, multiplying by
         10 three times in total)

     –   then multiply together the resulting whole numbers (4 × 12 = 48)

     –   finally divide the answer by 10 as many times as the numbers
         were multiplied by 10 altogether (48 → 0.048, dividing by 10
         three times).

◆   Note that the number of figures after the decimal points altogether
     in the numbers being multiplied is the same as the number you
     need after the point in the answer.

◆   Also be guided by the expected size of the answer (e.g. 4.1 × 0.5
     should be about 2).

Further practice

Do not use a calculator.

29.1 Find the value of $0.1 \times 0.2 \times 0.3 \times 0.4 \times 0.5$.

29.2 Expressed as a decimal, the proportion of pupils on free school meals in one school is 0.12. Of these pupils, the proportion who come from homes with no adults in employment is found to be 0.6. As a decimal, what proportion of pupils in the school are on FSM and are from homes with no adults in employment?

29.3 Rewrite and answer question 29.2 using percentages.

29.4 The A4 → A5 setting on the school photocopier reduces both the length and the width of the original by a scale factor of 0.71. By multiplying 0.71 by 0.71, find by what factor the area is reduced.

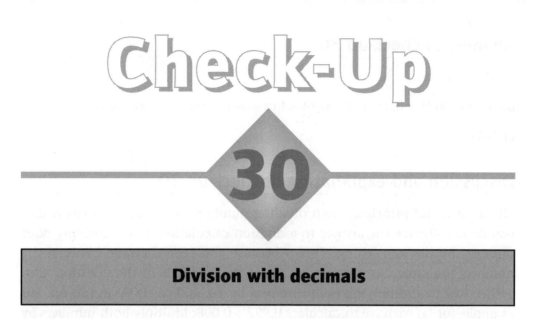

Check-Up

30

Division with decimals

Do not use a calculator.

a) In the GCSE music examination one year, 0.008 of the candidates were ungraded and 0.992 of the candidates achieved a grade. How many times more candidates achieved a grade than did not achieve a grade?

b) A sheet of A4 paper has an area of 0.0625 square metres. A sheet of A1 paper has an area of 0.5 square metres. Calculate 0.5 ÷ 0.0625 to find how many sheets of A4 can be cut from a sheet of A1.

c) For an illustration on a worksheet, a teacher wants to reduce a picture so that its height goes from 0.2 metres to 0.09 metres. Evaluate 0.09 ÷ 0.2 to find the scale factor to which the photocopier must be set for this reduction.

Answers to check-up 30

a) 124.

b) 0.5 ÷ 0.0625 = 8, so 8 sheets of A4 can be cut from a sheet of A1.

c) 0.45.

Discussion and explanation of check-up 30

The most useful principle when dividing numbers involving decimals is that you do not change the answer to a division calculation if you multiply both numbers by the same thing. This is because you keep the ratio between the numbers the same. So you can get rid of the decimals in the question altogether, just by multiplying both numbers by 10, 100 or 1000, and so on. For example, for (a) we have to calculate 0.992 ÷ 0.008. Multiply both numbers by 1000: 0.992 ÷ 0.008 = 992 ÷ 8 = 124. That's the answer, as simple as that! Notice that if the data in this question had been presented in percentages (0.8% and 99.2%), the calculation would have started as 99.2 ÷ 0.8 and multiplication by 10 would have produced the same result, 992 ÷ 8.

For (b), with the second number ending in the digit 5, I guess that the question will get easier if I double both numbers... and, as it happens, if I go on doubling, this particular question gets easier and easier: 0.5 ÷ 0.0625 = 1 ÷ 0.125 = 2 ÷ 0.25 = 4 ÷ 0.5 = 8 ÷ 1 = 8. So, a sheet of A1 is 8 times the area of a sheet of A4. The reason why you can actually cut 8 sheets of A4 from A1 is that the lengths and widths of the two paper sizes are also in the same proportion. This is true of all the A sizes, of course, with A0 having an area of 1 square metre, A1 being half of that, A2 half of that, and so on.

For (c), the scale factor required for the reduction (which must be less than 1) is 0.09 ÷ 0.2. Multiplying both numbers by 100 gets rid of the decimals and produces the equivalent calculation, 9 ÷ 20. To work this out, start with 9 ÷ 2 (= 4.5) and then divide this by 10 to get 9 ÷ 20 (= 0.45). The photocopier will probably display the scale factor as a percentage, i.e. 45% for 0.45.

Notice that when you divide by a larger number (20, rather than 2) you get a smaller answer. So, for example, the answer to 30 ÷ 0.6 will be 10 times *larger* than the answer to 30 ÷ 6. Check out these sequences, both starting with 30 ÷ 6, but one getting larger and the other smaller:

$30 \div 6 = 5 \rightarrow 30 \div 0.6 = 50 \rightarrow 30 \div 0.06 = 500 \rightarrow 30 \div 0.006 = 5000$, and so on.

$30 \div 6 = 5 \rightarrow 30 \div 60 = 0.5 \rightarrow 30 \div 600 = 0.05 \rightarrow 30 \div 6000 = 0.005$, and so on.

See also...

Check-up 33: Knowledge of metric units of length and distance

Check-up 34: Knowledge of metric units of area and solid volume

Check-up 37: Simplifying ratios

Summary of key ideas

◆ A division involving decimals (e.g. $0.68 \div 0.002$) can always be changed to an equivalent division with just whole numbers, by multiplying both numbers by 10 or by 100 or by 1000, and so on (e.g. $0.68 \div 0.002 = 680 \div 2$, multiplying both numbers by 1000).

◆ You can sometimes simplify the division by multiplying (or dividing) by other numbers (e.g. simplify $2.1 \div 0.35$, by doubling both numbers to give $4.2 \div 0.7$).

◆ If the divisor gets larger by a factor of 10, then the answer gets smaller by a factor of 10, and *vice versa* (e.g. $24 \div 4 = 6$, $24 \div 40 = 0.6$, $24 \div 0.4 = 60$).

Further practice

Do not use a calculator.

30.1 A teacher wants to enlarge a picture so that its width increases from 0.09 metres to 0.126 metres. Find the scale factor to which the photocopier must be set.

30.2 Which of the following gives the same result as $0.25 \div 85$?

    a) $0.5 \div 170$ b) $2.5 \div 8.5$ c) $25 \div 8500$ d) $0.025 \div 8.5$

30.3 Given that $34 \div 17 = 2$, write down the values of:

    a) $3.4 \div 1.7$ b) $34 \div 170$ c) $34 \div 0.17$ d) $0.034 \div 17$

Check-Up

31

Using approximations to check your answers

Do not use a calculator.

a) A classroom is 9.35 metres long, 7.95 metres wide and 2.45 metres tall. The volume in cubic metres is found by multiplying these lengths. There are 32 pupils in the class. Concerned about working conditions, a teacher uses a calculator to find the volume per pupil. Which of the following answers obtained in three attempts at this calculation is likely to be correct?

A 1.464   B 5.691   C 14.41

b) The numbers of Year 11 pupils attempting various GCSE subjects one year are shown in the table. The total number of Year 11 pupils was 581 195. Make a mental estimate of the approximate percentage of this total number entered for each subject.

English	French	Geography	History	Information Technology
533 080	312 990	217 407	190 213	86 789

Answers to check-up 31

a) B.

b) To the nearest percent, reading from the left, 92%, 54%, 37%, 33%, 15%. If your estimate is within 2% either side of these, well done!

Discussion and explanation of check-up 31

The purpose of this check-up is to encourage you to use approximating intelligently, particularly to check your written calculations or calculator work. It is very easy to press the wrong keys on a calculator or to get tripped up by its logic, so making a rough estimate of what the answer should be is important. I will try to explain the way I think about the calculations involved in this check-up.

In (a), we have first to find $9.35 \times 7.95 \times 2.45$. Approximately, 9.35×7.95 is about 9×8, but this is probably a bit of an under-estimate, because the 7.95 is only just short of 8, whereas the 9.35 is quite a bit more than 9. I could then approximate the 2.45 to 2, but this would be a further substantial under-estimate. So, I'm inclined to call it $2\frac{1}{2}$, which is a slight over-estimate, but which may compensate for the previous under-estimate. So, now I am working on $9 \times 8 \times 2\frac{1}{2}$, which is $9 \times 20 = 180$. Finally, we need to divide this by 32. Well, I know $180 \div 30$ is 6, so, remembering that increasing the divisor (from 30 to 32) decreases the answer, my guess is that $180 \div 32$ should be a bit less than 6. So I would expect the calculator result for this problem to be around 6, probably just under (option B). It is actually 5.691082, so my estimating has been very successful.

Example (b) illustrates a common situation where we will look at a table of data and mentally try to estimate the proportions involved as percentages. The first thing to do, of course, is to approximate the numbers involved, perhaps to the nearest ten thousand. I would then mentally think of the total number of pupils as 58 (ten thousands) and the other figures as 53, 31, 22, 19 and 9.

As usual, 10% and 50% are good starting points for mentally handling percentages. From 10% we can also find 90%. In this case 10% of 58 = 5.8 (just under 6), so 90% will be 58 – 5.8 = 52.2 (just over 52), and 50% = 29. The 53 for English is just over 52.2, so my estimate will be 91%. The 31 for French is 2 more than 29, so it should be 50% plus a bit. Since 2 is a third of 6, I'll go for an additional 3% (about a third of 10%), giving my estimate for French as

53%. The 22 for geography is 7 less than 50% (29), which I reckon to be about 12% less, giving my estimate for geography as 38%. The 19 for history is just 3 less than geography, which is about 5% less (since 10% is about 6), so I'll go for 33%. Then the 9 for IT is 6 + 3, which is about 10% + 5% = 15%.

See also...

Check-up 23: Mental calculations, finding a percentage of a quantity

---

Summary of key ideas

◆   Use approximating intelligently to make estimates of calculations, particularly to check calculator results.

◆   Round the numbers involved to just one or two figures, but try to balance over-estimates with under-estimates.

◆   When estimating percentages mentally, use 10%, 90% and 50% as starting-points.

Further practice

31.1 A teacher orders the following materials: 32 calculators at £3.79 each, 16 dictionaries at £8.45 each, 4 packs of overhead transparencies at £5.98 per pack, and 250 envelopes at 3.2p per envelope. VAT is to be added to everything except the dictionaries at the rate of 17.5%. Which of the following is a reasonable estimate for the total cost?

A £200   B £300   C £400   D £500

31.2 The numbers of Year 11 girls in England attempting various GCSE subjects one year are shown in the table. The total number of Year 11 girls was 287 450. Make a mental estimate of the approximate percentage of this total number entered for each subject.

English	French	Geography	History	Information Technology
266 765	163 145	95 107	97 200	33 990

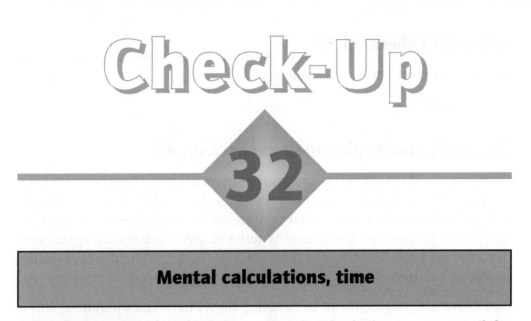

Check-Up

32

Mental calculations, time

Answer these questions using mental calculations, supported by whatever informal jottings you need.

a) A teacher records a science programme starting at 11.45 and finishing at 12.22, and a wild-life documentary starting at 19.25 and finishing at 21.00. How much time will be left on the four-hour video tape?

b) A junior school's daily timetable for taught sessions is 09.15–10.20, 10.45–12.35, 13.40–15.25. This operates five days a week, except for Wednesday when there is an additional school assembly from 11.55 to 12.35. What is the length of the taught week in hours, correct to one decimal place?

Answers to check-up 32

a) 108 minutes or 1 hour 48 minutes.

b) 22.7 hours.

Discussion and explanation of check-up 32

Obviously, in our professional lives as teachers we have to handle mental calculations of time with confidence and fluency. Most adults deal very competently with such calculations when they are set in a meaningful and purposeful context. By contrast, the questions posed in this check-up will appear artificial. My apologies for that, but some readers will appreciate the opportunity to practise the kind of contrived question that might be set in a numeracy test!

First, make sure you are fluent in handling the 24-hour clock notation. This is widely used in printed timetables, and generally disregarded – and therefore not reinforced – in spoken communications. The principle is easy enough to understand: we count in hours up to noon (12 hours, written 12.00) and then continue with 13 hours (13.00), 14 hours (14.00) and so on. Incidentally, when we get to midnight we start again with zero hours (00.00). The first two figures represent the hours and the last two represent the minutes past the hour. So, 18.12 is 12 minutes past 18 hours, or 12 minutes after 6 pm.

Calculations with time are best handled informally. The image of a time-line (like a number-line) is a useful device for working out time intervals between two times of day, often using the hours as convenient stepping-stones (compare Check-up 25). The diagram below shows how the recordings in (a) might be pictured. This total time taken is 15 mins + 22 mins + 35 mins + 1 hour = 2 hours 12 mins, which is 1 hour 48 minutes short of 4 hours.

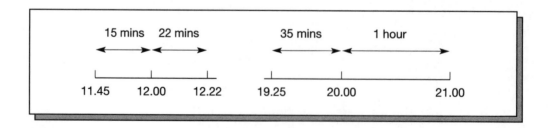

The daily timetable in (b), apart from Wednesday, can be pictured on a time-line as follows:

1 hour	5 mins		15 mins	1 hour	35 mins		20 mins	1 hour	25 mins

09.15   10.15 10.20 10.45   11.00   12.00   12.35   13.40 14.00   15.00 15.25

This gives the taught time for each day, apart from Wednesday, as 1 hour + 5 mins + 15 mins + 1 hour + 35 mins + 20 mins + 1 hour + 25 mins = 3 hours + (5 + 15 + 35 + 20 + 25) minutes = 4 hours 40 minutes. (Note that 15 + 20 + 25 = 60 minutes = 1 hour.) Wednesday is 40 minutes less than this, which is 4 hours. The total taught week then is 5×4 hours + 4×40 minutes = 20 hours + 160 minutes = 22 hours 40 minutes. As a fraction of an hour, 40 minutes is $\frac{2}{3}$, which as a decimal is 0.66666..., or 0.7 to one decimal place. So the total taught week is 22.7 hours. This is 0.8 hours short of the recommended 23.5 taught hours per week for Key Stage 2.

Summary of key ideas

◆   In the 24-hour clock notation for time, the first two figures represent the hours, starting from zero hours at midnight, and the last two figures represent the minutes after the hour (e.g. 15.25 is 25 minutes after 15 hours, which is 3.25 pm).

◆   Use the mental image of a time-line, with the hours as stepping-stones, to calculate time intervals between various times of day.

Further practice

Answer these questions using mental calculations, supported by whatever informal jottings you need.

32.1 A Year 4 class is to take the following tests during a morning: English comprehension, 55 minutes; mental arithmetic, 20 minutes; mathematics, 50 minutes. The school morning starts at 08.55, with break from 10.20 to 10.45, and finishes at 12 noon. A slot of 10 minutes is needed for registration and at least 5 minutes additional break must be given between papers. How would you organise the timetable?

32.2 A junior school's daily timetable for taught sessions is 09.20–10.55, 11.15–12.20, 13.25–14.20 and 14.35–15.30. This operates five days a week. What is the length of the taught week in hours? How close are they to the recommended 23.5 hours for Key Stage 2?

Check-Up

33

a) The length of a sheet of A4 paper is 297 mm. What is this in centimetres? What is it in metres?

b) The length of the school running track is 400 m. What is this in kilometres?

c) The speed limit on a German autobahn is 130 km/hour. What is this in miles per hour?

d) Which is longer, a 200-mm ruler or a 12-inch (foot) ruler?

Answers to check-up 33

a) 297 mm = 29.7 cm = 0.297 m.   b) 400 m = 0.4 km.

c) about 80 mph.   d) 12-inch.

Discussion and explanation of check-up 33

This check-up is an opportunity for you to make sure you have a basic knowledge of metric units of length and the relationships between them. The basic metric unit of length is the metre, which is about the distance from my nose to my outstretched finger-tip. Other units of length are then obtained by adding prefixes to this: such as, *kilo* (*k*) for a thousand, *centi* (*c*) for a hundredth and *milli* (m) for a thousandth. So, 1 km = 1000 m, 1 m = 100 cm, 1 m = 1000 mm, and 1 cm = 10 mm. Putting these another way: 1 m = 0.001 km, 1 cm = 0.01 m, 1 mm = 0.001 m = 0.1 cm.

So 297 mm = 29.7 cm (dividing by 10) and 297 mm = 0.297 m (dividing by 1000). Similarly, 400 m = 0.400 km (dividing by 1000).

Did you know that the distance from the North Pole to the equator is about 10 million metres? That's 10 000 km. Knowing this helps you to have some idea of distances on the Earth's surface. For example, the distance right round the equator would be about 40 000 km. It's always useful to learn by heart the lengths of a few items that you can use for reference like this. Start with your own height. I am 183 cm, for example – is that tall for a man, or average, or short? I always relate smaller lengths to the dimensions of A4 paper (297 mm by 210 mm, or about 30 cm by 21 cm). Most rulers used in school are 30 cm (300 mm) in length.

You should have some idea of how metric units relate to imperial units still in everyday use, like the mile. Most people use an approximation such as 5 miles = 8 kilometres or 3 miles = 5 kilometres. If you combine these you can get the following simple sequence of approximate conversions: 3 miles = 5 km, 5 miles = 8km, 8 miles = 13 km, 13 miles = 21 km, 21 miles = 34 km, 34 miles = 55 km, 55 miles = 89 km and so on. These are pretty good approximations and they can be used to work out other approximate conversions very easily. For example, knowing that 13 km = 8 miles (approximately) gives me 130 km = 80 miles, which is a reasonably accurate result.

You will find that inches are still widely used for many informal communications of lengths, even though officially nothing should now be sold in these imperial units. If you remember that a 12-inch ruler has been replaced by a 30-cm (300 mm) ruler, you should be able to convert between inches and centimetres fairly easily. The following are fairly good approximations which can be deduced from this starting-point: 15 cm = 6 inches, 10 cm = 4 inches, 5 cm = 2 inches, 2.5 cm = 25 mm = 1 inch.

See also...

Check-up 34: Knowledge of metric units of area and solid volume

Summary of key ideas

◆ Metric units of length include the metre (m), kilometre (1 km = 1000 m), the centimetre (1 cm = 0.01 m), and the millimetre (1 mm = 0.001 m).

◆ 1 m = 1000 mm, 1 m = 100 cm, 1 cm = 10 mm, 1 m = 0.001 km.

◆ Memorise the lengths of some reference items, such as the dimensions of A4 paper (about 30 cm by 21 cm), your height in centimetres, the distance from the North Pole to the equator (about 10 000 km).

◆ To convert between metric and imperial, remember: 3 miles is about 5 km, 5 miles is about 8 km; 30 centimetres is about 12 inches (one foot).

Further practice

33.1 The length of a sheet of A0 paper is about 1189 millimetres. Write this length in centimetres. Then write it in metres.

33.2 Estimate the following lengths:

a) the height of a standard litre-carton of milk, in cm

b) the length of a cricket pitch, in m

c) the diameter of the hole in the neck of a wine bottle, in mm.

33.3 If there was a motorway straight from the North Pole to the equator and you drove down it non-stop at 70 mph, about how long would the complete journey take? About how many degrees of latitude would you pass through per hour? (The whole journey is 90°.)

Check-Up

34

a) The area of a sheet of A0 paper is 1 m². Given that the length is about 1189 mm, use a calculator to find the width. A1 paper is half of a sheet of A0 paper. So what are the length and width of a sheet of A1? Now check that its area is 0.5 m².

b) The budget for a new school playing-field allows for a total area of 0.6 ha (0.6 of a hectare). Suggest some possible lengths and widths for a rectangular field of this size.

c) Without using a calculator, find how many rectangular boxes (cuboids), 25 cm by 50 cm by 20 cm, would fit into a metre-cube? What is the volume in m³ of one of these boxes?

Answers to check-up 34

a) A0 paper is approximately 1189 mm by 841 mm; A1 paper is about 841 mm by 594.5 mm.

b) 100 m by 60 m, 80 m by 75 m, 125 m by 48 m...

c) 40 boxes; the volume of one box is 0.025 m^3.

Discussion and explanation of check-up 34

The area of a rectangle is given by multiplying together the lengths of its two sides. If the two lengths are given in metres (e.g. 3 m by 4 m), then the area will be in square metres (12 square metres). The symbol for 'square metre' is m^2. My advice is to read this as 'square metre', not as 'metres square'. This language can otherwise cause confusion. For example, if you say 'five metres square' do you mean an area of 5 m^2 or a square of side 5 metres (which has an area of 25 m^2!). I would avoid the ambiguity by saying that a 5-metre square has an area of '25 square metres', while writing the area as 25 m^2.

For (a), since the area of the A0 paper is given in square metres (1 m^2) we start by writing the length in metres, as 1.189 m. Then the width is given by 1 ÷ 1.189 = 0.8410429 m (that's about 841 mm or 84.1 cm). The width of A0 becomes the length of A1. The width of A1 is half the length of A0, about 594.5 mm, or 0.5945 m. The area of A1 is therefore 0.8410429 × 0.5945 = 0.5 m^2, (approximately) or half a square metre. This relationship continues with other paper sizes: A2 (about 594.5 mm by 420.5 mm) has an area of 0.25 m^2 (a quarter of a square metre), and so on.

Units for larger areas include the *are (a)* and the *hectare (ha)*. An are is 100 m^2. Think of a 10-metre square (10 m × 10 m), which is about the size of a classroom. A hectare is 100 ares (the prefix *hecto* means a hundred), or 10 000 m^2. Think of a square field 100 m by 100 m. So an area of 0.6 ha is 6000 m^2. That could be a rectangular field with sides 100 m by 60 m, and so on. If you have a rural background you may have some sense of the size of an acre. So, just for reference, I might mention that an area of 200 m by 20 m is about an acre. That's 4000 m^2 or 0.4 ha.

One cubic metre (1 m^3) is the volume of a metre-cube; that's a cube with sides of 100 cm. This has a total volume of 100 × 100 × 100 = 1 000 000 cm^3

(a million cubic centimetres). In (c), assuming the width of the boxes is 25 cm, we could fit a row of 4 of these along one edge of a metre-cube. If each box is 50 cm long, we would then need 2 of these rows to make a layer of boxes covering the bottom of the metre-cube. That's 8 boxes in each layer. The height of each layer is 20 cm, so we could fit 5 layers into the metre-cube, giving us a total of 40 boxes. Writing the sides in metres, each box has a volume of $0.25 \times 0.5 \times 0.2 = 0.025$ m^3. (Note that $0.025 = \frac{1}{40}$.)

See also...

Check-up 33: Knowledge of metric units of length and distance

Summary of key ideas

◆   The area of a rectangle is found by multiplying together the lengths of the sides; but make sure these lengths are given in the same units.

◆   If the lengths are in metres (m), the area will be in square metres (m^2); if the lengths are in centimetres (cm), the area will be in square metres (cm^2); and so on.

◆   1 m^2 = 10 000 cm^2.

◆   The volume of a rectangular box (also called a cuboid) is found by multiplying together the lengths of the three sides; again make sure the same units are used for all three sides.

◆   If the lengths are in metres (m), the volume will be in cubic metres (m^3); if the lengths are in centimetres (cm), the volume will be in cubic centimetres (cm^3); and so on.

◆   1 m^3 = 1 000 000 cm^3.

◆   A hectare is 10 000 m^2, which is the area of a square field 100 m × 100 m.

Further practice

34.1 Measure the lengths of the sides of a sheet of A5 paper to the nearest millimetre. Check that these lengths give an area of about $\frac{1}{32}$ of a square metre.

34.2 A 1-litre carton of milk is a cuboid with sides approximately 17.5 cm, 9.5 cm and 6.5 cm. What is the volume in cubic metres of one of these cartons?

34.3 An acre is about 0.4 ha. About how many acres is a hectare? Suggest some possible lengths for the sides of a rectangular field with an area of 0.4 ha.

Check-Up

35

a) How much does a litre of water weigh, in kilograms?

b) A pupil has a 0.2-litre bottle of medicine for use at lunch-time. How many medicine-spoonfuls does this bottle hold?

c) In the medicine cupboard is a tube of 0.015 kg of hydrocortisone cream and an inhaler containing 100 micrograms (100 μg) of Ventolin. Write these two quantities in grams.

Answers to check-up 35

a) 1 kg.   b) 40.   c) 0.015 kg = 15 g; 100 µg = 0.0001 g.

Discussion and explanation of check-up 35

Liquid volume is usually measured in litres. A litre is the same volume as a thousand cubic centimetres. Imagine a cube with side 10 cm: that's the same volume as a litre! A kilogram is the weight of a litre of water. (NB: I use 'weight' in the colloquial sense. Some readers will be aware that we should say that a kilogram is the *mass* of a litre of water. For a discussion of the distinction, see chapter 22 of my book, *Mathematics Explained for Primary Teachers, 2nd edition, 2001*). Readers will be familiar with litre-cartons of milk and fruit juice. Since these materials are not very different in density from water – especially the economy range from the supermarket – if you put one of these cartons on the kitchen scales you will see that it registers about a kilogram or 1000 grams.

Units derived from the litre are: the millilitre, ml (1000 ml = 1 litre, 1 ml = 0.001 litres = a thousandth of a litre); the centilitre, cl (100 cl = 1 litre, 1 cl = 0.01 litres = a hundredth of a litre); the decilitre, dl (10 dl = 1 litre, 1 dl = 0.1 litres = a tenth of a litre). A miserly cup of coffee in the head's office would be about 1 decilitre (100 ml). The mid-morning mug of coffee in the staff-room would be about 2 decilitres (200 ml). The bottle of wine you drink when you get home from school may be labelled 750 ml, or 75 cl, or 7.5 dl, or 0.75 litres. You should get five 150-ml glasses out of this. The 0.2 litres in the medicine bottle is therefore 200 ml. Medicine spoons are usually designed for 5-ml doses, hence 40 spoonfuls in the bottle. If you feel more at home with pints than litres, then you should note that a pint is about 568 ml or 0.568 litres, or rather more than half a litre. Even though petrol is no longer sold in gallons, this old imperial measure still surfaces occasionally in conversation. So, for reference, a gallon is about $4\frac{1}{2}$ litres. Out of interest, ask your colleagues if they know roughly how many miles to the litre they can do in their car. I find that most people still talk about miles per gallon.

Since a kilogram is 1000 grams (1000 g), we can convert between the two by multiplying or dividing by 1000. So, for example, 0.015 kg = 15 g. The old imperial pound-weight is about 454 g, or 0.454 kg. Most produce that used to be sold in packs of one pound or half a pound are now sold in 500-g or 250-g packs. In (c) I have introduced another prefix, *micro*, symbolised by the Greek letter μ (mu). This stands for 'one millionth'. So a microgram, used for very small quantities, is 0.000001 g. The 100 µg in this question is therefore 100 × 0.000001 g = 0.0001 g.

See also...

Check-up 29: Multiplication with decimals

Check-up 30: Division with decimals

Check-up 52: Conversion graphs

Summary of key ideas

◆ Liquid volume is measured in litres: a litre is the same volume as 1000 cm^3.

◆ 1 litre = 10 dl (10 decilitres) = 100 cl (100 centilitres) = 1000 ml (1000 millilitres).

◆ 1 litre of water weighs the same as 1 kilogram (1 kg).

◆ 1 kg = 1000 g (1000 grams).

◆ A medicine spoon holds 5 ml; a wine bottle holds 750 ml.

◆ Some useful equivalents in imperial units: a pint is rather more than half a litre (about 568 ml); a gallon is about four and a half litres; a kilogram is rather more than two pounds (about 2.2 pounds).

Further practice

Do not use a calculator.

35.1 Purchasing factor 20 sun-screen prior to a class field-trip, a teacher has a choice of paying £6.50 for half a litre or £5 for 400 ml. Without using a calculator, decide which is the better buy.

35.2 A medicine bottle is labelled 1.25 dl. Write this volume in litres and then in millilitres. How many medicine-spoonfuls is this?

35.3 Which is greater: a) a quarter of a pound or 100 g? b) half a pint or 330 ml? c) 40 litres or 8 gallons? d) 10 stone or 70 kg? (1 stone = 14 pounds.)

35.4 Standard photocopier paper is 80 g per m^2. So, what is the weight of one sheet of A4 paper? What is the weight of a ream, in kg? Assuming an envelope weighs no more than four sheets, how many sheets of this paper can you confidently post with one first-class stamp (maximum weight allowed 60 g)?

Check-Up

36

Mental calculations, money

a) The exchange rate is about 12.5 Danish Kroner to the pound. About how much in pounds is it to buy tickets for 30 pupils to visit a museum in Copenhagen at 20 Kroner each?

b) How many tickets for the school concert at 75p each must we sell to raise £100?

c) Each pupil in a class of 30 requires a new textbook costing £4.40 and a workbook costing £2.50. What is the total cost?

d) A music teacher has £100 left in her budget. How many CDs at £6.95 each can she buy?

Answers to check-up 36

a) about £48.   b) 134.   c) £207.   d) 14.

Discussion and explanation of check-up 36

a) You could either convert the 20 kroner to pounds first and then multiply by 30, or multiply the 20 kroner by 30 first and then convert the answer into pounds. A good starting point is to note that since 12.5 kroner is about one pound, then 25 kroner is about £2 and 100 kroner is therefore about £8. (It's always a good idea to double when you have a 'point five' and to mutiply by 4 when you have 25 or 75 involved.) Here's a record of my mental calculations:

either: 100 kroner = £8, so 1 kroner = 8p (dividing by 100) and 20 kroner = £1.60

$$£1.60 \times 30 = £1.60 \times 10 \times 3 = £16 \times 3 = £48$$

or: $20 \times 30 = 600$. Total cost is 600 kroner $= 6 \times £8 = £48$.

b) One ticket raises 75p, so 4 tickets raise £3. (Note how multiplying by 4 is useful here.)

Now multiplying by 33, 132 tickets raise £99. $[4 \times 33 = (4 \times 30) + (4 \times 3) = 120 + 12 = 132]$

We're still £1 short, so we have to sell 2 more tickets to pass the target. That's 134 tickets in total.

c) Again, there's a choice here. Either we add up the cost of a textbook and a workbook and multiply the total by 30, or we multiply each one separately by 30 and then add up the results. Since I'm more likely to make a mistake in multiplication than in addition, I'll choose the first option, because it involves only one multiplication. This means working out £6.90 x 30. Now I'm attracted by the fact that £6.90 is 10p less than £7. So my mental reasoning is:

£7 × 30 = £210, 10p × 30 = £3, so total cost is £210 − £3 = £207

d) The CDs cost nearly £7 each. I happen to know that $7 \times 13 = 91$, so I start from this to get $7 \times 14 = 98$ (adding another 7). So for £98 I could buy 14 CDs at £7, with £2 change from the £100. This £2 plus the 14 extra five-pences (because they actually cost £6.95) is obviously not going to be enough to buy another CD.

See also...

Check-up 19: Rounding answers

Check-up 21: Mental calculations, multiplication strategies

Check-up 22: Mental calculations, division strategies

Summary of key ideas

◆   In doing calculations involving foreign currency, you can either do the exchange first and then the calculation, or the calculation first and then the exchange. Which is easier will depend on the numbers involved.

◆   If a multiplication or division involves 25, 250, 75 or 750, you can often make it easier by multiplying these numbers by 4.

◆   In informal mental calculations with money, always start from what you know and can handle with confidence.

Further practice

Do not use a calculator.

36.1 The exchange rate is about 2.5 Swiss francs to the pound. The 42 pupils going on a school trip are allowed £20 pocket money each. About how many Swiss francs is this in total?

36.2 How many marker pens costing £1.25 each can a teacher buy with an £18 gift token?

36.3 Each pupil in a school of 320 is to be provided with a lapel badge costing 24p and a notebook costing £1.50 for a school trip. How much will this cost to the nearest £10?

36.4 How many new textbooks costing £12.90 each can a teacher buy from a budget of £400?

Check-Up

37

Simplifying ratios

a) A primary school has 405 pupils and 18 teachers. Fill in the missing numbers, without using a calculator: 'In this school there are __ pupils for every 2 teachers, which gives a pupil–teacher ratio (PTR) of __:1.'

b) Use a calculator to find, to one decimal place, the PTR in a school with 790 pupils and 38 teachers, writing the ratio in the form __:1.

c) In a year's Ofsted inspections of primary schools, the arrangements for professional development of staff in 17% of schools were judged to be unsatisfactory. What was the ratio of schools judged unsatisfactory to those judged satisfactory or better in this respect? Use a calculator to express the ratio in the form 1: __, to one decimal place.

Answers to check-up 37

a) 45 pupils for every 2 teachers, so the PTR = 22.5:1.

b) 20.8:1.

c) 17:83 = 1:4.9.

Discussion and explanation of check-up 37

The language and notation of ratios are simply an extension of the ideas of fractions and proportions. But instead of comparing a part with the whole (as in '4 out of 10 teachers attend school assemblies'), we are comparing one quantity or number with another (as in 'for every 4 teachers who attend school assemblies, there are 6 who do not'). In this last example, we could express the *ratio* of those who attend to those who do not attend as 4:6, which is read 'four to six'. Ratios can be simplified in just the same way as fractions, by cancelling. So, for example 4:6 = 2:3.

Often, to get a feel for a ratio, it is useful to express it as 'one to something' or 'something to one'. So the ratio 2:3 might also be expressed as 1:1.5, meaning 'for every 1 who attends, 1.5 do not attend' or 'the number who do not attend is 1.5 times the number who do'.

In example (a) we have the ratio 405:18. Dividing both by 9, we get the equivalent ratio 45:2, which means '45 pupils for every 2 teachers'. Dividing the 45 by the 2 gives us the ratio as 22.5:1, which means '22.5 pupils per teacher'.

In example (b) we have the ratio 790:38. This does not cancel down easily to a much simpler equivalent form, so I would use a calculator to divide the 790 by 38 and express the ratio as 20.8:1. This means '20.8 pupils for every one teacher'. Of course, it does not mean that every teacher has 20.8 pupils in their class! But it does mean that (approximately) the number of pupils is 20.8 times the number of teachers.

In example (c) we have to compare the 17% judged unsatisfactory with the 83% (100% – 17%) judged satisfactory or better. The ratio is 17:83, meaning 'for every 17 unsatisfactory there were 83 satisfactory or better'. Because the 83 is the larger of the two numbers it makes more sense to divide the 83 by the 17, rather than the 17 by the 83, and thus to express the ratio as 'one to something'. The calculator gives me the ratio as 1:4.9, to one decimal place. This means 'the number of satisfactory or better was about 4.9 times the number of unsatisfactory'.

See also...

Check-up 38: Sharing a quantity in a given ratio

Check-up 39: Increasing or decreasing by a percentage

Check-up 41: Finding the original value after a percentage increase or decrease

Summary of key ideas

◆   The language and notation of ratios are used to compare one quantity or number with another.

◆   The ratio 3:7 is read as 'three to seven'.

◆   To say that the ratio of boys to girls is 3:7 means 'for every 3 boys there are 7 girls'.

◆   Ratios can be simplified by cancelling (for example, 36:84 = 3:7, cancelling 12).

◆   Ratios are often expressed as 'one to something' or 'something to one' (for example, 3:7 is approximately 1:2.3 and 85:34 = 2.5:1).

Further practice

37.1 A secondary headteacher's salary is £42,000 and a newly-qualified teacher's salary is £17,500. What is the *difference* in their salaries? Without using a calculator, find and simplify the *ratio* of their salaries. Write this in the form 'something to one'. How much does the head-teacher earn for every £1 that the NQT earns?

37.2 After a pay rise of 3.6%, the headteacher's salary is now £43,512 and the NQT's salary is £18,130. What is the difference in their salaries now? Use a calculator to express the ratio of their new salaries in the form 'something to one', to two decimal places.

37.3 After a further flat-rate salary increase of £500 per teacher, the head-teacher's salary is increased to £44,012 and the NQT's to £18,630. Now what is the difference in their salaries? And what is the ratio?

Sharing a quantity in a given ratio

a) A primary school headteacher has additional funding of £3640 to be distributed between the infant and junior sections of the school in the ratio 3:4. How much goes to each section? (No calculator needed.)

b) The governing body of a secondary school is concerned about the low ratio of young teachers (under 30) to older teachers and determines to improve this ratio from its current 1:4.5 to 1:3.5. How is the staff of 66 teachers currently distributed between young and older teachers? How will it be distributed if the target is achieved?

c) In the year 2000, the pupils who achieved GCSE passes at grade C or above in all four of English, mathematics, science and a modern foreign language were distributed between boys and girls in a ratio of about 5:7 in favour of girls. About what percentage were boys and what percentage girls?

Answers to check-up 38

a) £1560 to the infants, £2080 to the juniors.

b) Currently: 12 young, 54 older. Target: 14.67 young, 51.33 older.

c) 41.7% boys, 58.3% girls.

Discussion and explanation of check-up 38

In the examples in this check-up, there is a number or quantity that has to be split into two portions, in such a way that a particular ratio between the two parts is achieved.

In example (a), the £3640 has to be shared in the ratio 3:4. This means that if we divide it up into 7 equal parts, we have to give 3 of these parts to the infants and 4 of them to the juniors. Now, £3640 ÷ 7 = £520; so that's £520 × 3 = £1560 for the infants and £520 × 4 = £2080 for the juniors. Finally, we just check that the sums distributed do actually add up to the total we started with: £1560 + £2080 = £3640.

This example demonstrates the procedure for sharing a quantity in a given ratio. In general, to share Z in the ratio $a:b$, (i) divide Z by the sum of a and b; (ii) multiply the result separately by a and b to get the two shares; (iii) check that the results do add to Z.

Before the first step, it may also be helpful to simplify the ratio. So, in example (b), to share 66 teachers between young and older in the ratio 1:4.5, I would start by rewriting the ratio as 2:9, to get rid of the decimals. So we now divide the 66 by 11 (2 + 9), to get 6, and multiply this separately by the 2 and the 9, to get 12 young teachers and 54 older teachers. Check: 12 + 54 = 66.

Then, to deal with the target of 1:3.5, I would again simplify the ratio, to 2:7. Next we have to divide the 66 by 9 (2 + 7) and multiply separately by 2 and 7. Using a calculator for this, I get 14.666667 and 51.333333. You may suggest, reasonably, that these must be rounded to whole numbers (15 young and 51 older to pass the target). However, schools do employ a number of part-time teachers and teachers on job-shares, so calculations about staffing often involve fractions of teachers. So I have chosen to round the answers to 14.67 and 51.33. Check: 14.67 + 51.33 = 66.

Because 'percent' means 'out of 100', example (c) comes down to sharing 100% between boys and girls in the ratio 5:7. That's $100 \div 12 \times 5 = 41.7\%$ boys, and $100 \div 12 \times 7 = 58.3\%$ girls. Another way of looking at this is to say that $\frac{5}{12}$ of the pupils are boys and $\frac{7}{12}$ are girls, and then change these fractions to their percentage equivalents.

See also...

Check-up 18: Using a calculator to express a proportion as a percentage

Check-up 37: Simplifying ratios

Summary of key ideas

◆   To share a quantity or number Z into two portions in the ratio $a{:}b$ (e.g. share £24 in the ratio 3:5):

  – divide Z by the sum of a and b (£24 ÷ 8 = £3)

  – multiply the result separately by a and b to get the two shares (£3 × 3 = £9, £3 × 5 = £15)

  – check that the two shares add to Z (£9 + £15 = £24).

◆   If a quantity or number is shared in the ratio $a{:}b$ then the fraction in the first portion is $\frac{a}{(a+b)}$ and the fraction in the second portion is $\frac{b}{(a+b)}$ (for example, sharing in the ratio 3:5 results in $\frac{3}{8}$ in the first portion and $\frac{5}{8}$ in the second).

Further practice

38.1 The ideas in this check-up can also be applied to sharing quantities into three or more parts. For example, share a grant of £4800 between the nursery, infant and junior sections of a primary school in the ratio 1:2:5.

38.2 The entrants for GCSE music in the year 2000 were split between girls and boys in the ratio 4:3. What fraction of the entrants were boys and what fraction girls? Express the proportions of girls and boys as percentages of the total number of entrants. There were approximately 41 000 entrants. So, to the nearest hundred, about how many were girls and how many boys?

Check-Up

39

Increasing or decreasing by a percentage

a) The following prices are exclusive of VAT, which has to be added at $17\frac{1}{2}$%. What is the overall cost of each? Use a calculator only for the second example.

   i) A television monitor listed at £320

   ii) A printer listed at £196.50

b) A secondary school has 87 unauthorised absences in one term. To achieve at least a 12% reduction in this figure, what is the school's target for unauthorised absences the following term? Do this both without and with a calculator.

c) One year a primary school has 67% of pupils achieving level 4 or above in the Key Stage 2 English test. What would be their target for next year in order to increase this figure by 10 percentage points? What would be their target to increase it by 10%?

Answers to check-up 39

a) i) £376.   ii) £230.89.   b) 76.   c) 77%, 73.7%.

Discussion and explanation of check-up 39

Problems about percentage increases and decreases always contain three elements: the starting value, the percentage change and the finishing value. There are, therefore, basically three types of problems: (i) given the starting value and the percentage change, to find the finishing value; (ii) given the starting value and the finishing value, to find the percentage change; (iii) given the percentage change and the finishing value, to find the starting value. This check-up deals with the first of these. Check-ups 40 and 41 deal with the others.

a) To find $17\frac{1}{2}\%$, we can piece together 10%, 5% and $2\frac{1}{2}\%$, which is easy to do mentally for £320. 10% of £320 is £32, so (halving this) 5% is £16 and (halving again) $2\frac{1}{2}\%$ is £8. So the increase is £32 + £16 + £8 = £56, giving the finishing price as £376. The calculation of $17\frac{1}{2}\%$ of £196.50 is a bit tricky to do mentally, so we'll use a calculator. Now the obvious approach is to use the calculator to find $17\frac{1}{2}\%$ of £196.50 (see Check-up 24) and then use the calculator again to add this on to the £196.50. But there's a quicker way that I always use. When we have added on the $17\frac{1}{2}\%$ we will then have $117\frac{1}{2}\%$ of what we started with. So I can go straight to the finishing price just by calculating $117\frac{1}{2}\%$ of £196.50. I can do that on a calculator in just one step, by converting the percentage (117.5%) to a decimal (1.175), giving 196.50 × 1.175 = 230.8875, which rounds to £230.89.

b) You can find 12% of 87 mentally by piecing together 10%, 1% and 1%. That gives us 8.7 + 0.87 + 0.87 = 10.44. We will have to round this *up* to 11 to achieve the target reduction. Subtracting this from 87 gives the target as 76. Doing this with a calculator, we could say that the target for next term is 88% (100% − 12%) of the figure for this term. Since 88% = 0.88 we can do this just by entering this one calculation: 87 × 0.88. This gives 76.56, so the target is 76.

c) When the starting and finishing values are themselves percentages, there can be confusion when we talk about percentage changes. To increase the 67% *by 10 percentage points* means just to add 10% to the 67%, giving 77%. The 10%, 67% and 77% are all percentages of the whole quantity or set. But if we say that we aim to increase the score of 67% *by 10%* we mean that the 10% increase is 10% of the 67%, i.e. 6.7%. This gives a finishing figure of 67% + 6.7% = 73.7%.

See also...

Check-up 24: Finding a percentage of a quantity using a calculator

Check-up 40: Expressing an increase or decrease as a percentage

Summary of key ideas

◆   VAT at $17\frac{1}{2}$% can be found mentally by piecing together 10%, 5% and $2\frac{1}{2}$%.

◆   Many percentage increases and decreases can be calculated mentally by such informal methods (e.g. a decrease of 18% can be worked out as 10% + 5% + 1% + 2%).

◆   The finishing value after a percentage increase or decrease can be found on a calculator in one step (e.g. to increase by 27% multiply by 1.27; to decrease by 27% multiply by 0.73).

◆   If the starting and finishing values are themselves percentages, then increasing or decreasing by a number of *percentage points* is not the same as increasing or decreasing by a *percentage* (e.g. 80% decreased by 5 percentage points is 75%, but 80% decreased by 5% is 76%).

Further practice

39.1 In the Key Stage 1 writing task, 56% of a primary school's Year 2 pupils achieve level 2 or above. What would this be next year if the school were to achieve an increase of 5 percentage points? What would it be if this figure were increased by 5%? (No calculator required.)

39.2 What would you enter on a calculator to find the result of increasing 6543 by 21%? And what would you enter to find the result of decreasing 6543 by 21%?

39.3 A computer is listed at £789, to which must be added VAT at $17\frac{1}{2}$%. The firm offers schools a reduction of 12%. Would you prefer the VAT to be added first or the reduction to be applied first? Answer this intuitively and then use a calculator to work it out.

Check-Up

40

Expressing an increase or decrease as a percentage

a) (No calculator needed.) A school secretary's contract is increased from 80 hours per month to 100 hours. What is the percentage increase? A classroom assistant's contract is reduced from 100 hours to 80 hours per month. What is the percentage decrease?

b) (Use a calculator.) A primary school's average points score for science and mathematics in the Key Stage 2 statutory tests one year were 28.9 and 27.5 respectively. The following year they were 27.6 and 29.5 respectively. What were the percentage changes in the average points scores for science and mathematics?

c) The table below shows the percentages of pupils achieving level 5 or above in the Key Stage 3 mathematics statutory tests in England over five years. By how many percentage points have the numbers achieving this level increased between 1996 and 2000? What was the percentage increase in the number of pupils achieving this level over this period?

Year	1996	1997	1998	1999	2000
%	57	60	59	62	65

Answers to check-up 40

a) 25%, 20%.

b) About 4.5% decrease for science, 7.3% increase for mathematics.

c) 8 percentage points, which is about a 14.0% increase.

Discussion and explanation of check-up 40

In this check-up we look at problems where we are given the starting value and the finishing value and are required to find the percentage increase or decrease. It is important to remember that the increase or decrease is always expressed as a percentage of the *starting* value.

In example (a) the starting value for the secretary is 80, so the increase (20) is expressed as a proportion of 80. This is $\frac{1}{4}$ or a 25% increase.

But the starting value for the classroom assistant is 100, so the decrease (again 20) is this time expressed as a proportion of 100. Hence there is a 20% decrease. So, increasing from 80 to 100 is a 25% increase, but going from 100 to 80 is only a 20% decrease.

In example (b), the decrease for science is 28.9 – 27.6 = 1.3 points. This must be expressed as a proportion of the starting value, i.e., of 28.9. Using a calculator, 1.3 ÷ 28.9 = 0.0449827, or about 0.045, which is 4.5%. So the science score has decreased by about 4.5%.

The increase for mathematics is 29.5 – 27.5 = 2.0 points. This must be expressed as a proportion of the starting value, i.e., of 27.5. Using a calculator, 2.0 ÷ 27.5 = 0.0727273, or about 0.073, which is 7.3%. So the mathematics score has increased by about 7.3%.

In example (c) we are again dealing with values that are themselves percentages, so we must be aware of the distinction between the increase expressed in percentage points and the increase expressed as a percentage of the starting value (see Check-up 39). From 1996 to 2000 there is an increase of 8 percentage points in these figures, from 57 to 65. To express this increase as a percentage of the starting value, we calculate 8 ÷ 57 = 0.1403509, which is about 0.140 or 14.0%. So there has been about a 14% increase in the proportion of pupils achieving level 5 or above.

See also...

Check-up 39: Increasing or decreasing by a percentage

Check-up 41: Finding the original value after a percentage increase or decrease

Check-up 54: Substituting into formulas

Summary of key ideas

◆ Remember that an increase or decrease is always expressed as a percentage of the *starting* value (for example, a decrease of 10 from 50 to 40 is a 20% decrease because the 10 is 20% of the 50).

◆ To find a percentage increase or decrease using a calculator, just divide the increase or decrease by the starting value and read off the decimal answer as a percentage (e.g. if 48 increases by 3, calculate $3 \div 48 = 0.0625 = 6.25\%$).

Further practice

40.1 The price of a computer is increased from £1250 to £1400. Without using a calculator, what percentage increase is this? Later the price of £1400 is decreased by the same percentage. Do you expect the price now to be less than £1250, more than £1250 or equal to £1250? Answer this intuitively; then use a calculator to check.

40.2 (Use a calculator.) A secondary school's average points score for science and mathematics in the Key Stage 3 statutory tests one year were 31.6 and 32.9 respectively. The following year they were 31.8 and 31.1 respectively. What were the percentage changes in the average points scores for science and mathematics?

40.3 The table below shows the percentages of girls in Year 11 in England achieving five or more GCSE grades A*–C (or GNVQ equivalent) over five years. By how many percentage points has this proportion increased from 1996 to 2000? What is the percentage increase in the proportion of girls achieving these grades over this period? In which year from 1997 to 2000 was there the greatest percentage increase from the previous year in the proportion of girls achieving these grades?

Year	1996	1997	1998	1999	2000
%	49.4	50.0	51.5	53.4	54.4

Check-Up

41

Finding the original value after a percentage increase or decrease

a) (No calculator needed.) After a dramatic decrease of 20% from the previous year, a school roll stands at 664 pupils. What was it the previous year?

b) (Use a calculator.) Including VAT at 17.5%, a climbing frame costs £696.54. What is the price excluding VAT?

Answers to check-up 41

a) 830.   b) £592.80.

Discussion and explanation of check-up 41

These are the trickiest of the three kinds of problems involving percentage increases and decreases: when we have to work backwards from the finishing value and the percentage increase or decrease to find the starting value.

The situation in example (a) can be represented as follows:

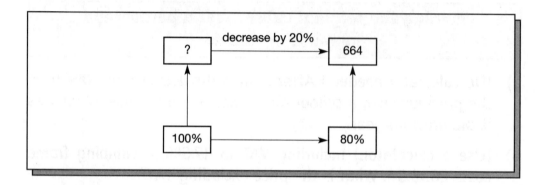

After the decrease by 20%, the finishing number of 664 is actually 80% of the starting number. To find the starting number we have to work back to 100% from 80% = 664. We can handle this informally like this:

80% = 664, which means 40% = 332 (halving), so 20% = 166 and
10% = 83. Hence 100% = 830

I would always start by trying to use informal calculations like this. It's a good way to build up your confidence with numbers.

But sometimes there is no obvious simple relationship between the numbers involved and we may have to resort to a calculator. This is the case in example (b). In this case we have to work back from the fact that 117.5% is £696.54 to find 100%. We can start by dividing by 117.5 to find what is 1% and then multiply by 100.

117.5% = £696.54, so 1% = £696.54 ÷ 117.5, so 100% =
£696.54 ÷ 117.5 × 100 = £592.80

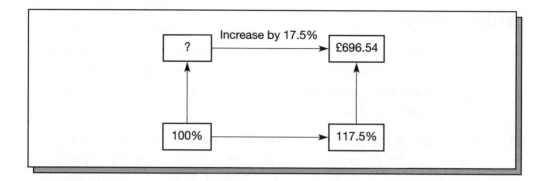

See also...

Check-up 39: Increasing or decreasing by a percentage

Check-up 40: Expressing an increase or decrease as a percentage

---

Summary of key ideas

◆ To find the starting value, given the finishing value after a percentage increase or decrease, write down what percentage the finishing value is of the starting value and work back to 100% (e.g. after an increase of 15% the finishing value will be 115%).

◆ Sometimes you can do this by informal methods (e.g. if 115% = £23, then 230% = £46, so 10% = £2 and 100% = £20).

◆ Other times you may need to use a calculator to find first 1% and then 100% (e.g. if 115% = 597, then 1% = 597 ÷ 115 and 100% = 597 ÷ 115 × 100).

Further practice

41.1 (No calculator needed.) One year, a primary school achieves a 26% increase in the proportion of pupils getting level 4 or above in the Key Stage 2 handwriting assessment. If the proportion this year is 63% what was it the previous year?

41.2 (Use a calculator.) There is concern expressed one year when a decline of about 14.2% from the previous year is reported in the number of pupils entering for GCSE music in England. If the figure entering this year is reported as 37 900, what was the figure the previous year, to the nearest hundred?

Check-Up

42

Calculating means

Two parallel mathematics classes in Year 7 took the same test. Their marks out of 50 were recorded as follows:

Class A: 43, 23, 26, 49, 40, 35, 37, 38, 25, 26, 47, 35, 38, 35, 33, 34, 39, 27, 29, 21

Class B: 32, 35, 38, 27, 32, 34, 23, 37, 21, 45, 42, 30, 40, 34, 32, 37, 21, 30, 29, 31, 20

Their teachers calculate the mean marks scored by each class in the test.

a) What is the mean mark of the pupils in Class A?

b) What is the mean mark of the pupils in Class B?

c) What can you deduce from the comparison of these two means?

Answers to check-up 42

a) 34.   b) 31.9.   c) very little.

Discussion and explanation of check-up 42

Given a set of data, such as those in this example, we often find it helpful to use some kind of figure that is representative of the whole set. Such a figure is called an *average*. The *mean* (also called the *arithmetic mean*) is a kind of average. To calculate the mean of a set of numbers, you simply add them all up and divide by however many of them there are. We might want to calculate the mean of a set of data for a number of reasons. For example, we might want to know how well a particular set of pupils is doing compared to some national norms or targets. Or, we might want to compare the performance of one group with another as part of an evaluation of some factor that we suspect might be related to their achievements.

The total of the scores for Class A is 680. There are 20 pupils in this class who took the test, so we divide this 680 by 20, giving the mean score to be 34. Imagine giving a counter to each pupil for each mark they score, then putting all the counters into a pot and sharing them out again equally between all the pupils. Each pupil would finish up with 34 counters. That's why the mean is calculated in this way and why it is used as one score to represent all the scores in the set.

The total of the scores for Class B is 670. There are 21 marks in this set. So the mean mark is 670 ÷ 21, which, using a calculator, comes to 31.9 (rounded to one decimal place). If you have to round a calculator answer, good practice is to give the value of the mean to one more decimal place than is used for the original numbers in the set. Since our set contains only whole numbers I have therefore rounded the mean to just one decimal place.

Comparing these two means we note that Class A achieved a higher mean score (34) than Class B (31.9) in this test on this occasion. But that's about all we can say. If the classes are parallel then we might expect the means to be about the same. But is 34 about the same as 31.9 or not? To judge whether the difference of 2.1 in their mean scores is significant we would have to examine the data more closely. We would consider, for example, the spread (dispersion) of scores achieved in the test. We might also gather more data about the classes' mathematical performance on a number of different occasions, using a range of assessment procedures. It also depends on what the reason is for finding the means.

See also...

Check-up 46: Measures of spread, range and inter-quartile range

---

Summary of key ideas

◆　An average is a value used as a representative figure for all the values in a set.

◆　The mean, also called the arithmetic mean, is one kind of average.

◆　To find the mean, add up all the values in the set and divide by the number of values.

◆　If you have to round the answer, give it to one more decimal place than is used for the values in the set.

◆　Be cautious in reading significance into comparisons based only on mean scores.

Further practice

42.1 School X has 12 classes, with the following numbers of pupils in them: 23, 35, 30, 32, 31, 29, 27, 28, 24, 26, 33, 25. School Y has 16 classes, with the following numbers of pupils in them:24, 25, 26, 28, 27, 31, 24, 28, 25, 24, 27, 29, 32, 30, 30, 24. Find the mean class-size for each of the two schools. Why might these means be calculated?

42.2 To evaluate the progress of their pupils from one national assessment to the next, schools are encouraged to calculate the 'average (mean) points score' for each subject in each assessment. The table shows the points awarded for each level in the Key Stage 3 English tests, as prescribed by the DfES Standards and Effectiveness Unit, and the numbers of pupils in one secondary school achieving these levels. Calculate the mean points score. When this statistic has been calculated, what kind of meaning does it have?

Level	3 or below	4	5	6	7	8	Exceptional performance
Points	21	27	33	39	45	51	57
No.of pupils	16	32	40	25	8	6	2

Check-Up

43

Modes

a) A school with pupils coming from 600 families does a survey of how many children there are in these families. They discover that the modal number of children is 3. Which of the following statements must be true?

i) At least 300 of the families have 3 children.

ii) There are more families with 3 children than any other number of children.

iii) The number of families with 2 children is less than the number with 3 children.

iv) There is a total of 1800 children in the 600 families.

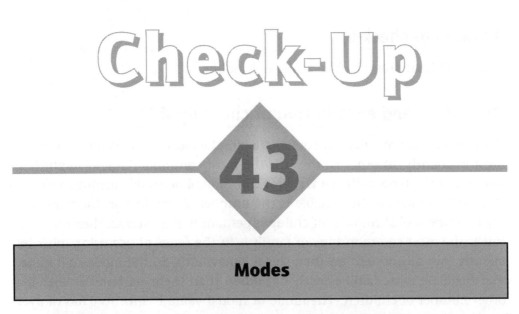

b) The graph above shows the number of families of pupils in a school owning various numbers of mobile telephones (0, 1, 2, 3, 4). What is the modal number of mobiles owned by these families?

Answers to check-up 43

a) ii) and iii) are true.   b) The mode is 1 mobile.

Discussion and explanation of check-up 43

If you have a set of values of some variable, the *mode* is the value that occurs most frequently. In other words, it is the most common value. It might help to connect the term with the French expression, *à la mode*, meaning 'fashionable'. In example (a) the variable is the number of children in the family. To say that 'the modal number of children per family is 3' means, therefore, that this is the most common type of family – in the sense of occurring most frequently (not a comment on their social behaviour!). So the mode of 3 means that there are more families with 3 children than there are families with any other number of children. The mode or modal value is another kind of average: one value that can in some way represent the whole set of values and enable us to make comparisons with other sets. The mode of 3 here, for example, suggests that this is an unusual population, since the modal number of children for most samples of UK families is 2. This is a good example of the use of a mode. It is most appropriate to use the mode when you are dealing with a fairly large population (in this case, the 600 families of children at the school) and discussing a variable that does not take many different values (in this case, the number of children per family).

Example (b) is another good example of the appropriate use of the mode, since there is a fairly large population (300 families) and a variable taking only five values (0, 1, 2, 3 or 4 mobiles). The modal value from the graph is easily spotted: it's the value of the variable with the highest frequency – the tallest column on the graph – i.e. 1 mobile.

The idea of a mode can also be used when there is a larger number of values of the variable, but where the data has been grouped, as in the table below. This shows the distribution of the marks out of 100 in a teacher-designed test for a year group of 90 pupils, but the results have been grouped into intervals, 0–9, 10–19, 20–29, 30–39, and so on. Note that the intervals are equal, each one covering a range of 10 marks. A quick glance at this table shows that the *modal interval* is the range 30-39. The teacher might have hoped to design a test with the modal range of scores in the sixties rather than the thirties – and might therefore use this simple observation of the modal interval to consider whether this test was actually appropriate for these pupils.

Marks	0–9	10–19	20–29	30–39	40–49	50–59	60–69	70–79	80–89	90–99
No. of Pupils	0	3	10	36	19	16	4	2	0	0

See also...

Check-up 7: Bar charts for grouped discrete data

Summary of key ideas

◆   Given a set of values of a variable, the mode is the value that occurs most frequently.

◆   The mode is another kind of average, a representative figure for the whole set that may enable comparisons to be made with other sets.

◆   The mode is useful for a fairly large population where the variable being considered takes only a small number of values.

◆   The idea of the mode can be extended to sets where the data has been grouped into intervals – the interval with the highest frequency is called the modal interval.

Further practice

43.1 The graph shows the percentages of pupils in a school achieving various levels (2, 3, 4, 5, 6) in the Key Stage 2 mathematics test. Which level is the mode?

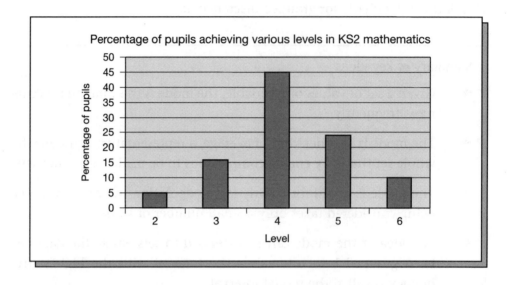

43.2 In Further Practice question 42.2, what was the modal level achieved by the pupils in the Key Stage 3 English assessment?

43.3 The table below shows the frequencies of various amounts of pocket money given weekly to pupils in a Year 5 class, grouped in intervals of £2. Which is the modal interval?

Amount	£0.00–1.99	£2.00–3.99	£4.00–5.99	£6.00–7.99	£8.00–9.99
No. of pupils	2	8	12	3	1

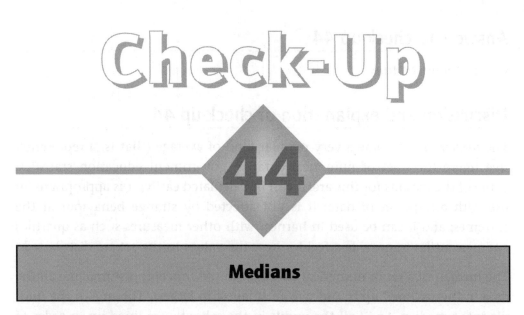

Check-Up

44

Medians

National data was collected to relate the achievement of pupils in England in the Key Stage 3 assessments in 1998 with their overall achievements in the year 2000 in GCSE/GNVQ examinations. This question refers only to those pupils who had a mean points score of 41 in the 1998 tests. For those pupils, the median points score in 2000 was found to be 60. Which of the following statements must be true for these particular pupils?

A   None of them scored more than 60 points in 2000.

B   More of them scored 60 points in 2000 than any other points score.

C   One of these pupils who scored 62 points in 2000 scored higher than at least 50% of them.

D   One of these pupils who scored 59 points in 2000 scored lower than at least 50% of them.

Answers to check-up 44

C and D must be true.

Discussion and explanation of check-up 44

The *median* has become a very popular kind of average (that is, a representative figure for a set of numerical data) in government education statistics. Some of the reasons for this are: it can be calculated easily; it is appropriate for use with a large set of data; it is not affected by strange behaviour at the extremes; and it can be used in harness with other measures such as quartiles and percentiles to provide a feel for how the values in the set are distributed.

The median of a set of numerical data is a simple concept. Just imagine all the data in the set lined up in order from smallest to largest. The one in the middle is the median. So, if all the pupils in the school were lined up in order of height, from the smallest to the tallest, the height of the pupil in the middle, say 148 cm, would be the median height. This means that someone who is taller than 148 cm is 'taller than average', in the sense that they are in the top 50% for height. Someone shorter than 148 cm is 'shorter than average' in the sense that they are in the bottom 50% for height.

In the example in this check-up, the median score is 60 points. This means that if all the pupils in this set were lined up in order from the lowest score to the highest, the pupil standing in the middle of the line would have a score of 60. (No doubt there will be a number of pupils either side of this pupil who have also scored 60.) Anyone scoring more than 60 points is therefore in the top half of scores and anyone scoring less than 60 points is in the bottom half. A pupil scoring 62 has definitely scored higher than at least 50% of the group. A pupil scoring 59 has definitely scored lower than at least 50% of the group. So, the median simply enables us to relate an individual value to the one in the middle. That's all it does!

People can get in a tangle trying to decide precisely where *is* the middle of a set of data. For a set of 99 items, for example, the middle one is clearly the 50th, because there are 49 other items either side of this one. But what about a set with an even number of items, such as 100 items? There isn't a middle item now. In this case, technically, the median is taken to be halfway between the *two* values in the middle, i.e. halfway between the 50th and 51st.

But, in practice, since the median is normally used for a large set of data, this is neither here nor there. The two values in the middle will probably be the same anyway.

See also...

Check-up 45: Upper and lower quartiles

Check-up 49: Percentiles

Summary of key ideas

◆ For a (large) set of numerical data, the median is the value of the item in the middle when they are arranged in numerical order from lowest to highest.

◆ A value higher than the median is greater than at least 50% of the items in the set.

◆ A value lower than the median is less than at least 50% of the items in the set.

Further practice

44.1 In the year 2000, in English non-selective schools with more than 50% of pupils known to be eligible for free school meals, the median percentage of pupils achieving grades A*–C for GCSE mathematics was 18%. What does this mean for a school with 52% of pupils eligible for FSM and 28% of their pupils achieving grade C or above in GCSE mathematics?

44.2 St Anne's School has English timetabled for $4\frac{3}{4}$ hours a week for its Year 3 classes, out of a total teaching timetable of $21\frac{1}{2}$ hours per week. National data indicates that the median percentage of the teaching week for all primary schools that is devoted to English in Year 3 classes is 25.0%. What does this tell us about St Anne's?

Check-Up

45

Upper and lower quartiles

This question also refers to the pupils and data described in Check-up 44. For those pupils, the lower and upper quartiles for the points scores in 2000 were found to be 54 and 65 respectively. Decide which of the following statements must be true for these particular pupils.

A   The middle 50% of these pupils scored in the range 54 to 65 in 2000.

B   All of these pupils scored in the range 54 to 65 in 2000.

C   One of these pupils who scored 66 points in 2000 scored higher than at least 75% of them.

D   One of these pupils who scored 64 points in 2000 was in the top 25%.

E   One of these pupils who scored 52 points in 2000 was in the bottom 25%.

Answers to check-up 45

A, C and E must be true.

Discussion and explanation of check-up 45

Quartiles are a simple extension of the idea of a median. Having lined up all the data in the set in order from smallest to largest, as well as identifying the one in the middle as the median, we identify the value a quarter of the way along the line as the *lower quartile* (LQ), and the value three-quarters of the way along the line as the *upper quartile* (UQ). So, the lower quartile, the median and the upper quartile divide the whole set into four quarters. Loosely speaking, we can think of the bottom quarter as being 'low', the top quarter as 'high', and the middle half as 'fairly average':

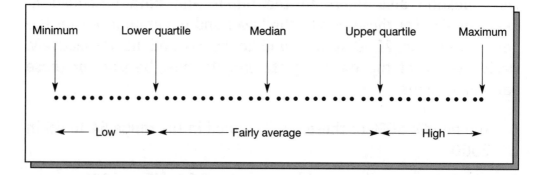

Using the heights of pupils in a year group as an example: those we might refer to as 'short' would have heights less than the LQ; those we might consider 'tall' would have heights greater than the UQ; and those of medium height, not especially short or tall, would lie in the range from the LQ to the UQ. If there were 15 items of data in a set, when the items are arranged in order, the LQ, the median and the UQ would be the 4th, 8th and 12th values. But, in practice you should not worry too much about how you would decide precisely where the lower and upper quartiles would be. Just think of them as being a quarter and three-quarters of the way along the list of data. These measures should only be used with fairly large sets of data anyway – and your main requirement will be to interpret these statistics rather than to find them.

So, in this check-up, knowing that the LQ and UQ are respectively 54 and 65 allows us to use these as reference points to identify whether a pupil has scored low, fairly average, or high, in relation to the others in the group. A score of 66 is above the UQ, putting this pupil in the 'high' group, or the top 25%. This score must exceed the scores of at least 75% of the pupils. At the other end, a score of 52 is below the LQ, putting this pupil in the 'low' group or the bottom 25%. This score must be exceeded by at least 75% of the pupils. A score of 64 is between the two quartiles, putting this pupil in the middle 50% of the whole group. In Check-up 44 we saw that this score of 64 is 'above average' in the sense that it is greater than the median. Reference to the quartiles allows us to go further and say something like 'above average but not in the top 25%'.

See also...

Check-up 46: Measures of spread, range and inter-quartile range

Check-up 47: Box-and-whisker diagrams

Check-up 48: More box-and-whisker diagrams

Check-up 49: Percentiles

Summary of key ideas

◆ For a (large) set of numerical data arranged in numerical order from lowest to highest, the lower quartile (LQ) is the value of the item a quarter of the way along the list, and the upper quartile (UQ) is the value of the item three-quarters of the way along the list.

◆ A value higher than the UQ is greater than at least 75% of the items in the set.

◆ A value lower than the LQ is less than at least 75% of the items in the set.

◆ We can think of the LQ and UQ as dividing the set into three sections: 'low' (the bottom 25%), 'high' (the top 25%) and 'fairly average' (the middle 50%).

Further practice

45.1 (This question is an extension of Further Practice question 44.1.) In the year 2000, in English non-selective schools with more than 50% of pupils known to be eligible for free school meals, the LQ, median and UQ for the percentages of pupils achieving grades A*–C for GCSE mathematics were 12, 18 and 25 respectively. What does this mean for a school with 52% of pupils eligible for FSM and 28% of their pupils achieving grade C or above in GCSE mathematics? What about another school with 52% FSM, but with only 15% of pupils achieving grade C or above in GCSE mathematics?

45.2 (This question is an extension of Further Practice question 44.2.) Data for all primary schools indicates that the LQ, median and UQ percentages of the Year 3 teaching week devoted to English are 22.2%, 25.0% and 28.1%. St Anne's Primary School devotes 22.1% of the Year 3 teaching week to English. What does this tell us about St Anne's? What about St Michael's School, that devotes 30% of its Year 3 teaching week to English?

Check-Up

46

Measures of spread, range and inter-quartile range

A teacher gave the same Year 10 science test, marked out of 100, to successive cohorts (A and B) and summarised their scores in the table below. The median scores were about the same for the two cohorts. But which had the greater range of scores? Compare the spread of scores using the inter-quartile ranges (IQRs).

	Minimum	Lower quartile	Median	Upper quartile	Maximum
Cohort A	23	45	56	63	91
Cohort B	40	46	57	78	90

Answers to check-up 46

Cohort A (range = 68 marks) had a greater range than Cohort B (range = 50 marks).

Cohort B (IQR = 32) had a greater IQR than Cohort A (IQR = 18).

Discussion and explanation of check-up 46

To compare sets of data like these, we need to look not just at 'average' figures like the median and the mean, but also at how the values in the sets are spread. In one case we might find that all the values are tightly clustered around the average compared to another in which they are much more greatly dispersed. There are four commonly-used measures of dispersion in statistics: the range, the inter-quartile range, the variance and the standard deviation. You may come across the last two, for example in data provided with standardised tests, but they are too technical for this book.

The difference between the minimum and the maximum is called the *range*. The *range* in Cohort A, for example, is 91 – 23 = 68. Note also that sometimes we might just say that the range of values is from 23 to 91. The range is a useful starting point for discussing spread. The range in Cohort A is much greater than that in Cohort B, suggesting much more variability in performance in Cohort A. However, the larger range of scores in Cohort A might be due to just one or two unrepresentative individuals who scored exceptionally high or exceptionally low. Because of this, the *inter-quartile range* (IQR) is a better indicator of spread. The IQR is just the difference between the LQ and the UQ. Since this excludes the top 25% and bottom 25% of marks, it tells us how spread out are the scores of the middle 50% of pupils in the cohort. In our example, the IQR in Cohort A is 63 – 45 (= 18), and the IQR in Cohort B is 78 – 46 (= 32). This means that, excluding the pupils who scored high and those who scored low in the test, the scores of the middle 50% of pupils in Cohort B were more greatly spread out than those of the middle 50% of pupils in Cohort A.

The five statistics given in the table – the minimum, the LQ, the median, the UQ and the maximum – provide what is sometimes called a 'five-number summary' of the data. The diagram below shows these numbers represented on a number line, with the range and IQR being the lengths of the arrows indicated.

| Minimum | Lower quartile | Median | Upper quartile | Maximum |

Range

IQR

See also...

Check-up 47: Box-and-whisker diagrams

Check-up 49: Percentiles

Summary of key ideas

◆ The range and the inter-quartile range (IQR) are two simple ways of measuring the extent to which data in a set is spread.

◆ The range is just the difference between the maximum and minimum values.

◆ The IQR is the difference between the upper and lower quartiles.

◆ The IQR is not affected by a few exceptionally high or low values at the extremes.

Further practice

46.1 A survey of a large sample of primary schools reports the following data about the number of hours devoted per week to PE and RE in their Key Stage 1 classes:

Hours per week	Minimum	Lower quartile	Median	Upper quartile	Maximum
PE	0.5	1.0	1.2	1.7	2.2
RE	0.5	0.9	1.1	1.3	1.8

Compare the ranges and inter-quartile ranges for this data.

Check-Up

47

Box-and-whisker diagrams

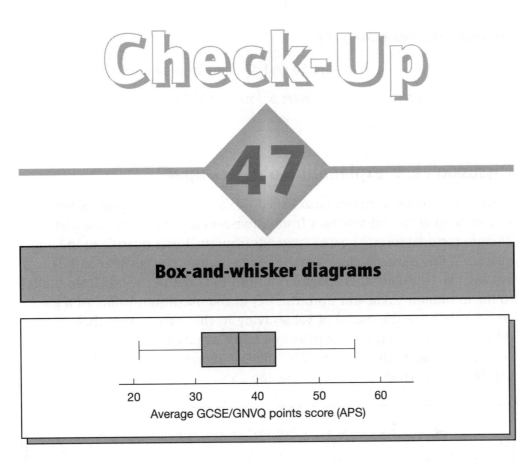

The box-and-whisker diagram above provides information about the spread of average points scores (APS) in GCSE/GNVQ examinations for about 3200 maintained mainstream secondary schools in England in one particular year.

a) What was the median value of the APS for these schools?

b) What were the highest APS and the lowest APS achieved by any school?

c) What was the range of APSs for the 1600 or so schools in the 'fairly average' bracket?

d) How well did a school with an APS of 28 do compared to all schools nationally?

e) About how many schools had an APS of 43 or more?

Answers to check-up 47

a) about 37.   b) about 56 and 21.   c) from about 31 to 43.

d) in the bottom 25%, i.e. they were a 'low-scoring' school.

e) about 800 schools at least.

Discussion and explanation of check-up 47

A box-and-whisker diagram (also called a box-and-whisker plot) is simply a way of putting the information from a five-number summary (see Check-up 46) into pictorial form. The 'box' extends from the lower quartile to the upper quartile. A line is usually drawn in the box to indicate the position of the median. The two 'whiskers' then extend out from the sides of the box from the LQ to the minimum value and from the UQ to the maximum value. At a glance you can then see the spread of values lying in the three groups that we have referred to in previous check-ups as low, fairly average and high. The left-hand whisker represents the bottom 25%, the box represents the middle 50% and the right-hand whisker represents the top 25%.

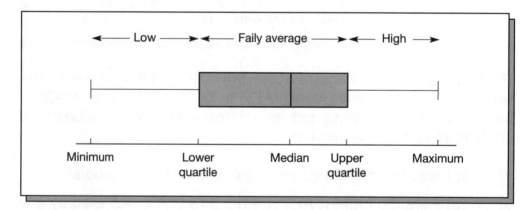

I have chosen to draw these diagrams with the scale going horizontally. You will also see them drawn vertically, but the principles are just the same.

Looking at the diagram in the check-up on the previous page, I can read off that, in terms of APS, the bottom 25% of schools (i.e. roughly the bottom 800 schools) had scores ranging from about 21 to 31. The middle 50% of schools (i.e. roughly the middle 1600 schools) had scores ranging from about 31 to 43. The top 25% (i.e. roughly the top 800 schools) had scores ranging from about 43 to 56. We cannot be too precise in reading off this information. The point of the diagram is to give a quick overview, at a glance, of the distribution of scores. I can't tell from the diagram, for example, whether the scores of the top 800 schools were spread across the whole range from 43 to 56, or whether 799 of them scored 43 and just one scored 56!

A particular school can then look at the data represented in this form and identify their position in relation to the results nationally. A school with an APS of 28 is in the left-hand whisker, clearly in the bottom 25%. A school with an APS of 32 is in the box, the middle 50%, but well below the median. A school with an APS of 38 is pretty much in the middle, definitely 'fairly average'. A school with an APS of 48 is clearly in the high-scoring, top 25%.

These box-and-whisker diagrams are often used for making comparisons between sets of data, by drawing two or more such diagrams side by side, as in Further Practice question 47.1.

See also...

Check-up 48: More box-and whisker diagrams

Summary of key ideas

◆ A box-and-whisker diagram is a picture of the way in which the values in a set of numerical data are distributed, using the minimum, the LQ, the median, the UQ and the maximum values as reference points.

◆ The box extends from the LQ to the UQ and represents the middle 50% of the set.

◆ One whisker extends from the LQ to the minimum value and represents the lowest 25% of the set.

◆ The other whisker extends from the UQ to the maximum value and represents the highest 25% of the set.

Further practice

47.1 The diagram shows the distributions of marks out of 100 in literacy and numeracy tests given to about 200 Year 7 pupils on entry to a secondary school. Are the following statements basically valid or invalid inferences from this data?

A At least one pupil scored 100 marks for numeracy, but no pupil scored 100 marks for literacy.

B The median marks for literacy and numeracy were about the same.

C Nine pupils scored higher in numeracy than in literacy.

D A boy scoring 40 in both tests did equally well in literacy and numeracy compared to other pupils.

E A girl scoring 70 in both tests did better in numeracy than in literacy relative to other pupils.

F In general, these pupils found the numeracy test harder than the literacy test.

G The lowest 100 literacy scores ranged from 20 to 40.

H There was a much greater spread of scores in the top 25% for numeracy than for literacy.

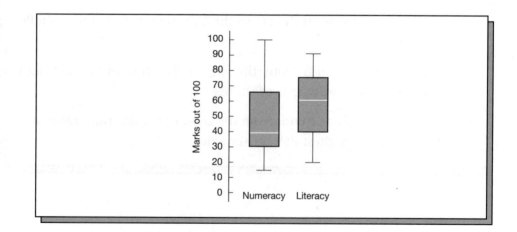

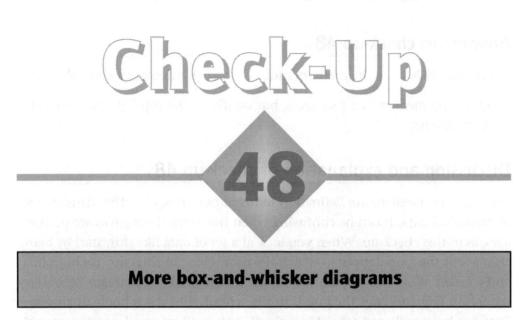

More box-and-whisker diagrams

The diagram shows the range of performance in GCSE examinations one year for all maintained mainstream schools in England, based on the percentages of pupils in the school achieving grades A*–C for each of the three core subjects.

a) For which of the three subjects was the median percentage of pupils achieving grades A*–C the highest?

b) For which subject did the bottom 25% of schools have percentages of pupils gaining these grades in the range 10–27%?

c) For which two subjects were there broadly similar distributions of percentages of pupils gaining grades A*–C across the schools?

d) Compared to results nationally, how well did a school perform for which the proportions of pupils gaining A*–C grades were 59% for English, 57% for mathematics and 53% for science?

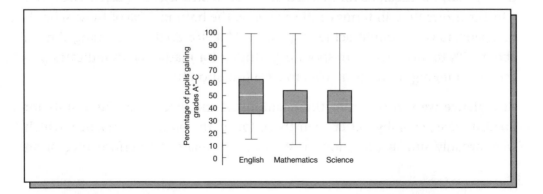

Answers to check-up 48

a) English (50%).   b) mathematics.   c) mathematics and science.

d) above the median in all subjects, but clearly in the top 25% of schools for mathematics.

Discussion and explanation of check-up 48

Quartiles and medians are defined in terms of percentages of the items in a set of numerical data. It can be confusing when the items themselves are percentages, as in this check-up. When you look at a set of data like this, start by being clear about the 'population' to which the data refers. In this case, for both box-and-whisker plots the population is 'all maintained mainstream secondary schools in England': not the pupils in the schools, but the schools themselves. Data has been collected school by school, not pupil by pupil, to generate this diagram. The second thing to be clear about is the *variable* being used to distinguish between the members of the population. In this case, the variable for each box-and-whisker plot is different: the percentage of pupils achieving grades A*–C in English, the percentage in mathematics, and the percentage in science. Each school has supplied a value for each of these variables.

The box-and-whisker plot for English shows that, for all maintained mainstream secondary schools in England (the population), the percentage of pupils achieving grades A*–C (the variable) ranged from a minimum of about 15% to a maximum of 100%. The top whisker shows that, in terms of this variable, the top 25% of these schools had percentages for English that ranged from about 63% to 100%. The box shows that the middle 50% of schools had percentages for English ranging from about 36% to 63%. The median percentage for English is 50%, indicated by the line in the box. This is greater (question a) than the medians for mathematics (41%) and science (42%). The lower whisker shows that, in terms of this variable, the bottom 25% of these schools had percentages of pupils achieving grades A*–C for English that ranged from about 15% to 36%. The corresponding whisker for mathematics indicates percentages ranging from about 10% to 27% (question b).

At a glance we can see from the positions of the boxes that the results for English were generally better than those for mathematics and science, which were broadly similar (question c). We can also relate the performance of an individual school very easily. The school with 59% for English and 53% for science is above the median, but not above the upper quartile for these subjects. But their 57% for mathematics puts them clearly into the top whisker, i.e. in the top 25% of schools in terms of the proportion of pupils achieving grades A*–C for this subject.

See also...

Check-up 49: Percentiles

Summary of key ideas

◆ When interpreting a box-and-whisker diagram, first identify clearly the *population* to which the data refers and then the *variable* being used to distinguish between them.

◆ If the variable is itself a percentage, then be careful not to get confused between the values of the variable and the percentages of the population represented by the box and by the whiskers.

Further practice

48.1 The diagram presents data about the performance in one year of schools in England with Year 6 pupils, in the Key Stage 2 English national assessment. It compares schools with 8% or less pupils eligible for free school meals (about 5000 schools) with those with more than 50% (about 1000 schools), in terms of the percentages of pupils achieving level 4 or above in English.

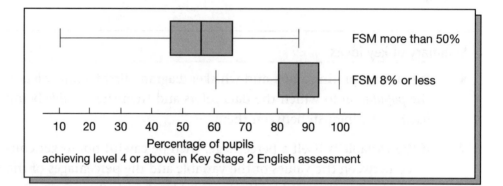

a) What is the population to which each of these box-and-whisker plots refers? What is the variable used to distinguish between members of these populations?

b) Precisely what information is communicated by the right-hand whisker on the bottom? And what by the box on the top?

c) What does the diagram tell you at a glance about the comparative achievements of the two populations of schools in the English Key Stage 2 assessments?

d) Hay Primary School has 7% of pupils eligible for FSM and has 75% of their Year 6 pupils achieving grade 4 or above in English. Lock Junior School has 52% of pupils eligible for FSM and also has 75% of their Year 6 pupils achieving grade 4 or above in English. Comment on the performances of these two schools in relation to national results.

Check-Up

49

Percentiles

The table presents data provided by the DfEE about the percentages of pupils achieving level 6 or above (6+) in the Key Stage 3 national tests in the year 2000 in mathematics and science, for all maintained mainstream schools in England with Key Stage 3 pupils.

	95%	UQ	60%	Median	40%	LQ	5%
Maths	90	52	43	38	33	26	12
Science	76	38	30	26	21	15	5

a) What is the population to which this data refers and what are the variables used to distinguish between members of this population?

b) What is the meaning of the 90 in the maths row?

c) Interpret the column headed 60%.

Answers to check-up 49

a) Population: all maintained, mainstream schools in England with Key Stage 3 pupils. Variables: the percentage of pupils gaining level 6+ in the Key Stage 3 mathematics tests in the year 2000 – and the same for science.

b) For maths, the top 5% of schools had 90% or more of their pupils gaining level 6+.

c) The 60th percentiles were 43% and 30% for maths and science respectively. The top 40% of schools in each subject had at least these proportions of pupils gaining level 6+.

Discussion and explanation of check-up 49

The table in this check-up is typical of many such tables that appear in government education statistics. It is difficult to interpret because the variables involved in each row of data are themselves percentages (of pupils). The headings 95%, 60%, 40% and 5% refer to percentages of *schools*, but are actually shorthand for the 95th, 60th, 40th and 5th *percentiles* (%iles).

Percentiles are an extension of the ideas behind quartiles and the median (Check-ups 44 and 45), providing further reference points in a large set of data. Imagine all the data lined up in order from smallest to largest. So, in the case of science in this example, in our mind we might have the headteachers of all the schools in a line, holding up cards showing the percentage of their pupils that gained level 6+ in Key Stage 3 science. On the left would be the school with the lowest percentage and on the right the school with the highest. We now work along the line until we come to the school that is 5% of the way along. For example, with about 3200 schools in the line this will be round about school number 160. Think of the percentage written on this school's card as the 5th percentile. According to the table it is (confusingly) 5%. When we get to 40% of the way along the line (round about school number 1280) we can think of the percentage written on this card as the 40th percentile, which in this case is 21%. And so on for other percentiles. Note that the LQ is the 25th percentile, the median is the 50th %ile and the UQ is the 75th %ile. Perversely, but typically, the table in this check-up has the 95th percentile first and the 5th last as we read from left to right.

The 60th percentile for science is 30%. What this means precisely is: if we ranked all the schools (the population) according to the proportions of their pupils gaining level 6+ for science (the variable), the top 40% of schools would have proportions of 30% or more – and the bottom 60% of schools would have proportions of 30% or less. If the science proportion for my school is 31%, then the data allows me to infer that we are in the top 40% of schools, but not in the top 25%.

See also...

Check-up 45: Upper and lower quartiles

Summary of key ideas

♦   Percentiles are used as reference points in a large set of data.

♦   If the members of the population are ranked from lowest to highest values of the variable, think of the 40th percentile as the value that is 40% of the way along the line.

♦   The bottom 40% of the members in this ranking would have values up to the value of the 40th percentile.

♦   The top 60% would have values from the 40th percentile up.

♦   The LQ, median and UQ are the 25th, 50th and 75th percentiles.

Further practice

49.1 The table presents data provided by the DfEE about average points scores in the Key Stage 1 national assessments in the year 2000, for maintained mainstream schools in England with Key Stage 1 pupils (about 16 000 schools).

	95%	UQ	60%	Median	40%	LQ	5%
Reading	18.3	16.9	16.2	15.8	15.4	14.6	12.7
Writing	16.6	15.3	14.7	14.3	13.9	13.2	11.3

    a) What is meant by the 16.2 in the row for reading?

    b) Clarendon Primary School had an average points score of 16.7 for both reading and writing. How did they do in relation to national results?

    c) About how many schools achieved a points score of 18.3 or more for reading?

49.2 *Deciles* are based on the same idea as percentiles, but the set is divided into *tenths* rather than hundredths. So, for example, the 60th percentile could be called the 6th decile and the 2nd decile is the 20th percentile. Interpret the following statement: 'For non-selective secondary schools with more than 5% and up to 9% of pupils eligible for FSM, the 9th decile for the proportions of pupils gaining grade C or above in GCSE science was 69%'.

Check-Up

50

The assessment coordinator in a primary school used an Excel worksheet to present in a scatter graph the results of the 20 pupils in Year 5, from standardised tests in each of maths and English.

a) How many pupils scored over 120 in maths? In English? In both?

b) How many pupils achieved higher scores in maths than in English?

c) What were the scores of the pupil who had the biggest difference between maths and English scores?

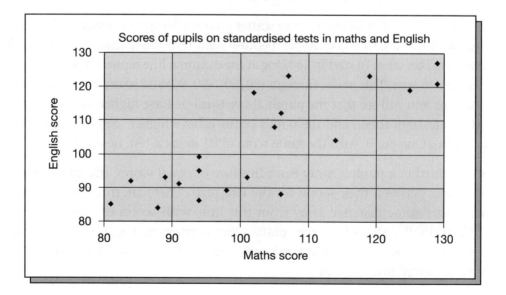

Answers to check-up 50

a) 3, 4, 2.   b) 9.   c) 106 for maths and 88 for English.

Discussion and explanation of check-up 50

Scatter graphs are used to relate two variables for a given population. In this example, the 'population' is the set of 20 pupils in Year 5 in this school. The two variables, represented by the scales on the two axes, are the score in the standardised English test and the score in the standardised mathematics test. Each member of the population, i.e. each pupil, is represented by a dot on the graph. The data provided in this check-up is invented, but it is fairly typical of what you might get in such tests. Typically, these tests are designed so that for the population at large the mean standardised score will be 100 and the standardised scores of most pupils (about 95%) will be in the range 70 to 130. Looking at the graph provided here, the 9 dots to the left of the vertical 100 line represent the pupils who scored less than 100 for mathematics. The 11 dots below the horizontal 100 line represent the pupils who scored less than 100 for English.

a) To locate the pupils who scored more than 120 in mathematics, look to the right of the vertical line passing through 120 for maths. There are 3 of them. For the pupils who scored more than 120 in English, look above the horizontal line passing through 120 for English. There are 4 of them. To locate the pupils who scored over 120 in both, look in the rectangle in the top right-hand corner. There are 2 pupils in this region.

b) The purpose of putting data into scatter graphs is to see the relationship between the two variables. In this example, because both tests are standardised in the same way, it makes sense to start by looking at the diagonal line representing equal scores on the two tests. This passes through (80, 80), (90, 90) and so on. Place a ruler along this line. You will see that the pupils above this line have higher scores for English (there are 10 of them) and the pupils below it have higher scores for maths (nine of them). One pupil, with the same score of 91 in each test, lies on the line.

c) The further a pupil is away from this line of equal scores, the greater the discrepancy between their scores for the two tests. There are three pupils who are obviously some distance away from this line, with scores of (102, 118), (107, 123) and (106, 88), where the maths score is given first and the English score second. The last of these has the largest difference in scores and is actually the furthest away from the line.

See also...

Check-up 5: Two-way tables for comparing two sets of data

Check-up 51: Scatter graphs and correlation

Summary of key ideas

◆   A scatter graph is used to relate two variables for a given population.

◆   Each variable is represented by a scale along one of the two axes.

◆   Each member of the population is represented by a dot on the graph.

Further practice

50.1

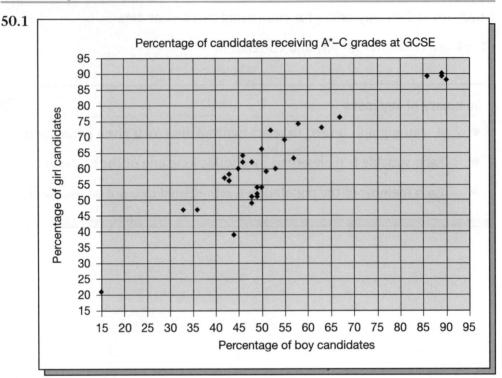

The scatter graph uses national data from the 1999 GCSE results for 31 subjects to compare the performances of boy and girl candidates from Year 11 classes.

a) In how many of these subjects did more than 65% of boy candidates gain grades A*–C?

b) In how many of these subjects did more than 65% of girl candidates gain grades A*–C?

c) In how many subjects were the percentages of both boys and girls gaining grades A*–C under 45%?

d) In how many subjects was the percentage of girl candidates achieving grades A*–C higher than that for boys?

e) What was the biggest difference between the percentages for boys and girls in one subject?

Check-Up

51

Scatter graphs and correlation

The table provides data from a sample of 16 secondary schools, showing the percentage of their Year 11 pupils entered for a GCSE in a modern language and the percentage of these candidates getting grades A*–C.

% entry	60	63	68	71	78	80	83	83	85	88	89	89	90	90	91	91
% A*–C	58	59	67	62	47	59	45	40	48	41	46	44	52	48	39	33

Plot these results in a scatter graph. Does there appear to be any correlation? Is it positive or negative? Is it broadly the case that the schools with a higher proportion of entries have a lower percentage gaining grades A*–C?

Answers to check-up 51

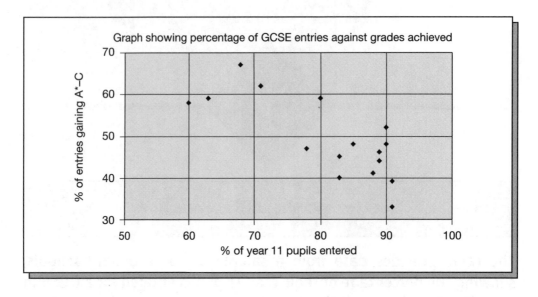

There appears to be a negative correlation. Generally, the higher the percentage of entries, the lower the percentage of grades A*–C, and *vice versa*.

Discussion and explanation of check-up 51

Scatter graphs are often used to see at a glance if there is any *correlation* between the two variables involved. If there is a *positive correlation* then there will be a tendency for the points on the graph to be clustered around a diagonal line sloping upwards. This indicates that, broadly speaking, as one variable increases so does the other. This does not have to be true for all the data, just a general tendency. A *negative correlation* occurs when there is a tendency for the points to be clustered around a diagonal line sloping downwards, as in this example. If the points are just generally scattered here and there, then there is probably no correlation between the two variables. These ideas are, of course, more appropriate to larger sets of data than to this example.

Here's a simple way to identify a correlation. Draw two vertical lines on the graph, one with about a quarter of the points to the right and the other with about a quarter of the points to the left and with the remaining half of the points between them. Do this for the scatter graph above. The data is divided into three sections: low, medium and high, in terms of percentage of pupils entered. Now draw two horizontal lines, one with about a quarter of the points above and the other with about a quarter of the points below, and the remaining half of the points between them. In our example, these lines would divide the data into low, medium and high in terms of percentage of pupils gaining grades A*–C.

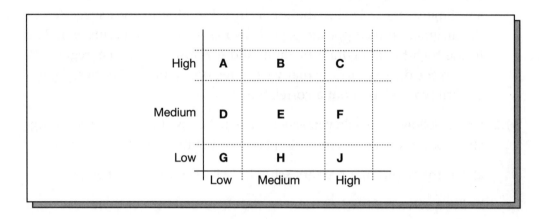

This produces nine regions on the scatter graph, as shown in the diagram. If there is a positive correlation, then the majority of the points should lie in regions G, E and C, with very few in regions A and J. If there is a negative correlation, then the majority of points should lie in regions A, E and J, with very few in regions G and C. In this example, there are 10 out of 16 points lying in A, E and J, with no points in G and C, confirming that there is a negative correlation between the two variables here.

Summary of key ideas

◆   A positive correlation between the two variables in a scatter graph is indicated when the points are clustered around a diagonal line sloping up.

◆   A negative correlation is indicated when the points are clustered around a diagonal line sloping down.

◆   A positive correlation means that there is a *tendency* for one variable to increase as the other increases, and for one to decrease as the other decreases.

◆   A negative correlation means that there is a *tendency* for one variable to increase as the other decreases, and *vice versa*.

Further practice

51.1 Does the scatter graph in Check-up 50 indicate a positive correlation, a negative correlation or no correlation between the scores in the maths and English tests? Divide the graph into the nine regions suggested in the diagram on the opposite page. How many of the 20 points would lie in the high-high, medium-medium and low-low regions (i.e. regions C, E, G in the diagram)? How many lie in regions A and J? Do these figures confirm your view about a correlation?

51.2 For the following, would you expect there to be a positive correlation, a negative correlation, or no correlation between the two variables suggested?

a) For the pupils in a primary school, their ages and their heights.

b) For a cohort of teacher-trainees, the circumferences of their heads and their scores in a numeracy test.

c) For the pupils in a secondary school, the number of minutes after 7 o'clock they leave home for school, and the distance they live from the school.

Check-Up

52

Conversion graphs

No calculator to be used.

Assume that you can exchange 1 pound sterling for 1.60 euros.

Mark one point on the diagram provided to represent the exchange of £100 into euros. Then draw a line that will enable you to make other conversions. Use the graph to find approximately (a) how many euros you would get for £85, and (b) the cost in pounds of 36 filled baguettes priced at 2.50 euros each.

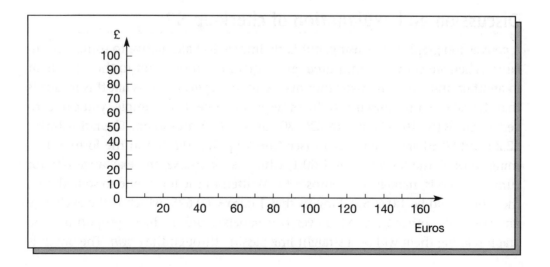

Answers to check-up 52

The point (160,100) shows the exchange of 160 euros for £100. Draw a line from (0,0) to (160,100).

a) The dotted line from £85 shows that this can be converted to about 136 euros.

b) The dotted line from 90 euros (36 × 2.50 = 90) shows that this is equivalent to about £56.

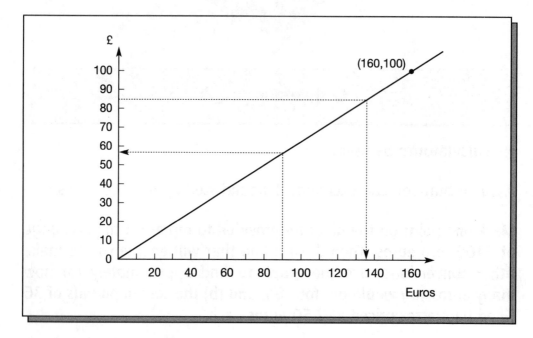

Discussion and explanation of check-up 52

A conversion graph is a pleasing, but fairly impractical alternative to using a calculator. When we convert a measurement or quantity in one unit to the equivalent in another unit, then the two amounts are in *direct proportion*. What this means is that the ratio of one amount to the other is the same. For example, you can convert 16 euros to £10, 32 euros to £20, 80 euros to £50, and so on. The ratios 16:10, 32:20 and 80:50 are all equivalent (see Check-up 37). Written in the form 'something to one', the ratio here is 1.60:1, which is, of course, the exchange rate for euros to pounds, namely 1.60 euros = £1. Written in the form 'one to something', the ratio would be 1:0.625, telling us that 1 euro = £0.625, which is the exchange rate going the other way. Whenever two variables are in direct proportion, the graph relating them will be a straight line passing through the *origin*. The origin is where the axes meet, the point with coordinates (0,0). This point represents, in our case, the obvious fact that zero pounds can be exchanged for zero euros.

The slope (or gradient) of the line is the amount it goes up vertically for one unit horizontally. Since you get 0.625 pounds for every extra euro, then 0.625 is the gradient. In general, if the ratio between the variable on the horizontal axis and that on the vertical axis is 1:m, then m is the gradient. In the example above, the ratio was 1:0.625. If the exchange rate changes and the value of the pound increases against the euro, then the graph will have to be redrawn with a steeper gradient. If the value of the pound falls, then the gradient gets less steep. If Britain signs up to adopt the euro before you read this book, then much of this discussion will appear irrelevant!

See also...

Check-up 36: Mental calculations, money

Check-up 37: Simplifying ratios

Summary of key ideas

◆ Converting a quantity or measurement from one unit to an equivalent amount in another unit is a process of direct proportion.

◆ Two variables that are in direct proportion (such as an amount in pounds and the equivalent in some other currency) produce a straight-line graph passing through the origin.

◆ The slope or gradient of the graph is m, where 1:m is the ratio between the variable on the horizontal axis and that on the vertical axis.

◆ The gradient is the amount the line goes up for every one unit moved horizontally.

Further practice

52.1 Use the conversion graph provided in the answers to Check-up 52 to find the cost in pounds of hiring in France a coach for which the price is quoted as 140 euros.

52.2 Which of the following pairs of variables would be in direct proportion and would produce a straight-line graph passing through the origin:

a) the weight of a letter in grams and the corresponding cost of postage in pence

b) the length in m of the side of a square field and the area of the field in m^2;

c) the weight of a person measured in pounds and their weight measured in kg

d) the National Curriculum level achieved by a specific pupil in mathematics assessments from Year 1 to Year 11, and the year group of the pupil.

52.3 A length of 100 inches is about 254 cm. Imagine drawing a conversion graph for inches to centimetres, with centimetres along the horizontal axis and inches along the vertical axis. Give the coordinates of two points through which the straight-line graph must pass. What would be the gradient of the line?

Interpreting pie charts

A governing body aimed over a two-year period to take the opportunity presented by some early retirements to adjust the age profile of the staff of a school more in favour of younger teachers. The data presented in the pie charts puts the teachers in the school into age groups of 20–29, 30–39, and so on, based on the age in years at the beginning of the school year. Was the aim of the governing body achieved?

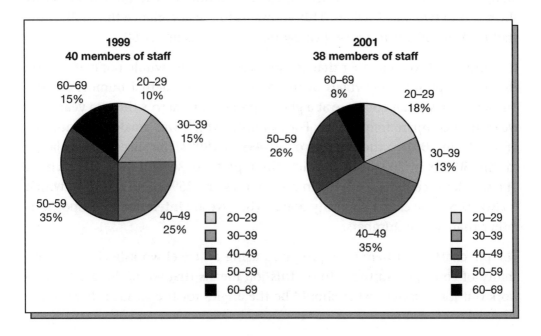

1999
40 members of staff

60–69 15%
20–29 10%
30–39 15%
50–59 35%
40–49 25%

Key: 20–29, 30–39, 40–49, 50–59, 60–69

2001
38 members of staff

60–69 8%
20–29 18%
50–59 26%
30–39 13%
40–49 35%

Key: 20–29, 30–39, 40–49, 50–59, 60–69

Answers to check-up 53

Yes, it was achieved. The proportions of teachers in the 60–69 and 50–59 sectors reduced; the proportion of 20–29s increased. In 1999 the 50–69 bracket was half the staff; in 2001 it was only about a third. There was, however, a marked increase in the proportion of staff in their forties.

Discussion and explanation of check-up 53

A pie chart is a useful way of presenting a set of frequency data where the 'population' to be represented is clearly divided into a fairly small number of discrete, non-overlapping subsets. Each member of the population must belong to one and only one of these subsets. The whole pie then represents the whole population and the sizes of the sectors (slices) represent what proportions of the whole population are in the various subsets. In this example, for the pie chart on the left, the 'population' is the staff of the school in 1999. The whole pie represents all 40 teachers. The subsets are the teachers in their twenties at the start of the school year, those in their thirties, and so on. There are only five of these subsets, making this data ideal for presentation in a pie chart.

At a glance we can see the proportions in the various groups. The 40–49s are clearly one quarter of the staff. This is confirmed by the percentage written alongside, 25%. The vertical line down the middle of the pie conveniently slices it into two equal halves. This allows us to see at a glance that half of the staff is in the 50–59 and 60–69 categories and half is under 50.

It is important to remember that the pie represents the whole population and the slices represent *proportions* of the population, not actual numbers or frequencies. So, we can compare at a glance proportions across the two years, but we cannot compare frequencies. For example: which was greater, the number of 50–59s in 2001 or the number of 40–49s in 1999? The slice of pie is larger for the 50–59s in 2001. But this actually represents 26% of 38 = 10 teachers. The smaller slice for the 40–49s in 1999 represents 25% of 40 teachers, which is also 10. So, pie charts are really useful when we are interested in proportions rather than actual numbers.

The pie charts used here were produced using an Excel worksheet. The availability of computer software to do this job means that we no longer have to work out for ourselves what should be the angles for the various slices of the pie. But remember that the total angle at the centre is 360°, half the pie uses 180°, and a quarter has an angle of 90°, also known as a right angle. Half of that, a slice of 45°, represents an eighth of the population. These are useful at-a-glance reference points when looking at a pie chart. Look out also for thirds (120°) and sixths (60°).

See also...

Check-up 6: Bar charts and frequency tables for discrete data

Summary of key ideas

◆   The whole pie in a pie chart represents the whole population for which data is provided.

◆   Each slice represents a discrete subset of the population.

◆   The size of the slice represents the proportion of the population within that subset.

◆   A pie chart should be used for discrete data with a fairly small number of subsets.

Further practice

53.1 Which of these might sensibly be represented in a pie chart?

a) The proportions of pupils in a primary school gaining level 4 or above in Key Stage 2 tests over a period of five years.

b) Information about the proportions of pupils in a school with various ethnic origins.

c) The distribution of 1300 pupils across the 52 classes of a secondary school.

53.2 This pie chart below shows how the 240 pupils in a primary school travelled to school one morning in the summer term. Fill in the missing words.

a) About a _____ of the pupils came by car.

b) The proportion of pupils who came by bike or walked was nearly a _____.

c) More pupils came by _____ than came by car.

d) A total of 48 pupils came by _____.

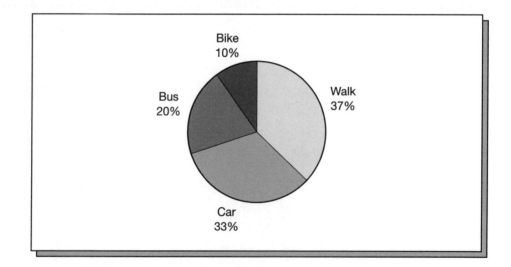

Check-Up

54

Substituting into formulas

The average points score for Key Stage 3 English for a school is calculated using the following formula:

$$\frac{57A + 51B + 45C + 39D + 33E + 27F + 21G}{A + B + C + D + E + F + G}$$

where A is the number of pupils achieving exceptional performance, B, C, D, E, F are the numbers at levels 8, 7, 6, 5, 4 respectively, and G is the number at level 3 or below.

Using a calculator if necessary, find the average points score for a school where A = 3, B = 10, C = 15, D = 40, E = 30, F = 10 and G = 7.

Answers to check-up 54

The average points score is 37.6, to one decimal place.

Discussion and explanation of check-up 54

To interpret this formula, remember that in algebra it is common practice to omit multiplication signs, because they can be confused with the letter X. So, 57A means 57 multiplied by the value of the variable A. In this example, A = 3, so 57A = 57 × 3 = 171. It is also more usual to use fraction notation to represent division, rather than the division symbol. So, for example, P/Q would mean P ÷ Q. In this example, we have a long expression on the top of the fraction to be divided by another long expression on the bottom.

When substituting actual values for the variables in a formula, remember the algebraic rules about precedence of operators (see Check-up 15). In this example, we have to do the multiplications on the top first, before the additions. Because the fraction line runs under the whole of the expression on the top, it tells us to work all of that out first, before dividing. So, the division line also acts like a bracket. The addition on the bottom can be done mentally, to get the total of 115.

Using a basic four-function calculator with a memory, the key sequence for finding the value on the top would be: MRC, MRC (to clear the memory), 57 × 3 = M+, 51 × 10 = M+, 45 × 15 = M+, 39 × 40 = M+, 33 × 30 = M+, 27 × 10 = M+, 21 × 7 = M+. This calculates each product and successively adds the results into the memory. Now recall the total from the memory and divide by 115: MRC ÷ 115 =, giving the required value for the average points score.

What this formula is actually doing is simply to find the *mean* points score for Key Stage 3 English for all the pupils involved. The formula on the bottom gives the total number of pupils. The formula on the top gives the sum of all their points scores for English: 3 scores of 57 (57 × 3), 10 scores of 51 (51 × 10), and so on. Dividing the total points scored by the total number of pupils gives the mean.

Substituting specific values for the variables in a formula is straightforward provided you do the operations in the order prescribed by the formula, giving precedence to brackets, divisions and multiplications. Also, if the formula involves units, be careful that the values you substitute are in the right units.

For example, a plumber's charges in pounds might be given by the formula 0.4T + 35, where T is the time spent in minutes. You will get a nasty shock when the bill arrives for a 2-hour job if you had substituted T = 2, instead of T = 120!

See also...

Check-up 15: Using a four-function calculator, precedence of operators

Check-up 17: Using the memory on a four-function calculator

Summary of key ideas

◆   When substituting specific values for the variables in a formula, be careful to do the operations in the order prescribed by the formula, giving precedence to brackets, divisions and multiplications.

◆   In algebraic notation, the multiplication sign is usually omitted (e.g. 7Q means $7 \times Q$) and fraction notation is normally used for division (e.g. 7/Q means $7 \div Q$).

Further practice

54.1 The formula for converting temperatures from Celsius (centigrade) to Fahrenheit is $F = 32 + 9C/5$, where F is the temperature in degrees Fahrenheit and C is the corresponding temperature in degrees Celsius. To convert the other way the formula is $C = 5(F - 32)/9$.

a) To the nearest whole number, what is F when C = 16?

b) To the nearest whole number, what is C when F = 82?

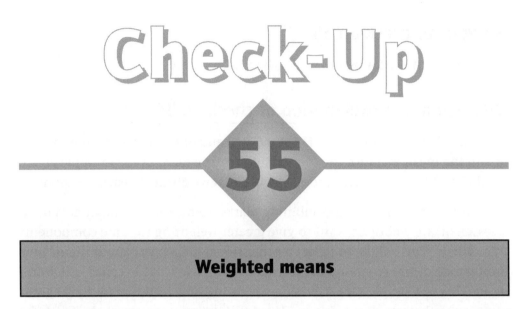

Check-Up

55

Weighted means

The assessment of a sixth form music course combines marks out of 100 for three coursework tasks, harmony (H), analysis (A) and composition (C), with the examination mark (E), to give an overall mark for music (M). The marks for harmony, analysis, composition and examination are given weightings of 1, 2, 3 and 4, respectively.

a) Write down a formula for calculating M.

b) Find the overall mark for a student whose marks are: H = 68, A = 64, C = 50, E = 42.

Answers to check-up 55

a) M = (H + 2A + 3C + 4E)/10.   b) 51.4.

Discussion and explanation of check-up 55

If we added up the four marks (H + A + C + E) and divided by 4, then we would obtain the mean mark for the four components, which, in the example given, would be 224 ÷ 4 = 56. This process gives equal weighting to each component.

However, particularly when combining marks from various components of an assessment, we will often want to give greater weighting to some components than others. This will be to reflect a professional judgement about the relative importance of the components. In this case we use what is called a *weighted mean*. This is a simple idea. Giving a weighting of 2 to the mark for analysis just means that we count this mark twice. Similarly, we count the mark for composition three times and the mark for the examination four times. So, effectively, it is as though there are, in this example, *ten* marks for which we have to find the mean: H, A, A, C, C, C, E, E, E, E. So we add these up and divide by *10*.

So the process for finding a weighted mean is to multiply each individual component by its weighting (H, 2A, 3C, 4E), add up the results (H + 2A + 3C + 4E) and then divide this by the sum of the weightings (1 + 2 + 3 + 4 = 10). Hence M = (H + 2A + 3C + 4E)/10.

Using a basic four-function calculator with a memory, the appropriate key sequence for the calculation in (b) would be:

MRC, MRC (to clear the memory), 68 M+, 64 × 2 = M+,
50 × 3 = M+, 42 × 4 = M+, MRC ÷ 10 =

This gives the weighted mean as 51.4, which is substantially lower than the equal-weighting mean of 56. The reason for this is clearly that this student has achieved lower marks on the components carrying greater weighting.

If the same four marks had been achieved, but with the higher marks for the components with greater weighting, the overall mark would have been higher. For example, H = 42, A = 50, C = 64, E = 68 gives M = 60.6.

See also...

Check-up 56: Combining means or percentages from two or more sets of data

---

Summary of key ideas

◆ A weighted mean is a process for combining numbers, such as marks in assessment components, so that greater weight is given to the components judged to be more important.

◆ To calculate a weighted mean, multiply each individual component by its weighting, add up the results, and then divide by the sum of the weightings.

Further practice

55.1 For teacher assessment of a pupil's National Curriculum level in mathematics at Key Stage 2, a weighted mean for the levels achieved in the four mathematics attainment targets has to be calculated, using these weightings:

AT1   Using and applying mathematics   2

AT2   Number and algebra   5

AT3   Shape, space and measures   2

AT4   Handling data   1

The result must then be rounded to a whole number, with halves rounded up.

a) Using A, B, C, D as variables representing the levels achieved for AT1, AT2, AT3, AT4 respectively, write down a formula for the overall level, L.

b) A pupil in Year 5 is assessed as being just at level 4 for AT2, and at level 3 for each of AT1, AT3 and AT4. What is this pupil's overall level for mathematics?

c) A year later this pupil has made excellent progress, has consolidated the level 4 for AT2, has reached level 5 for AT1 and for AT3, and made it to level 4 for AT4. What is the pupil's overall level now?

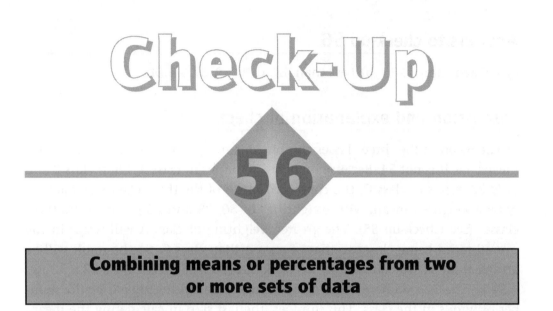

Check-Up

56

Combining means or percentages from two or more sets of data

Do not use a calculator.

a) The mean mark out of 50 achieved in a spelling test by the 30 pupils in class A was 35. The mean mark for the 28 pupils in class B was 34 and the mean mark for the 22 pupils in class C was 33. Was the overall mean for the three classes equal to 34? Greater than 34? Less than 34?

b) There are more boys than girls in a Year-9 cohort. If 50% of the girls and 46% of the boys achieve level 5 or above in English, will the proportion overall of pupils achieving this level be equal to 48%? Greater than 48%? Less than 48%?

c) On a car journey from Norwich to Birmingham and back again, I average 50 mph on the outward journey and 30 mph on the return journey. What is my overall average speed?

Answers to check-up 56

a) Greater than 34.   b) Less than 48%.   c) 37.5 mph.

Discussion and explanation of check-up 56

a) The mean of the three classes combined is not just the average of the three means, i.e. it is not 34. Because there are 30 pupils in class A, 28 in class B and only 22 pupils in class C, the combined mean of the three classes will actually be a weighted mean, with weightings of 30, 28 and 22 given to the three classes (see Check-up 55). The greater weighting of class A will result in the overall mean being closer to that of class A than class C. So the result will be greater than 34. To calculate it, we work out $(30 \times 35 + 28 \times 34 + 22 \times 33)/80 = 34.1$. The 30×35 here is the mean score for class A multiplied by the number of pupils in the class. This 'undoes' the last step in calculating the mean, where we divide the total of their marks by the number of pupils. So, 30×35 gives the total marks for class A. Similarly, 28×34 and 22×33 give the total marks for classes B and C. Add these up and we get the total marks for all three classes. To get the overall mean, this total has to be divided by the number of pupils in the three classes ($30 + 28 + 22 = 80$).

b) The same process is involved in finding a combined percentage arising from putting two or more sets together. The larger set has a greater weighting in calculating the percentage for the combined set. To get a feel for this, imagine an extreme example for this question. Say there are 1000 boys in the cohort and only 2 girls. The 46% of the boys is 460 boys, the 50% of the girls is just 1 girl! That's a total of 461 pupils out of 1002 gaining level 5 or above. As a percentage this will not be very different from the boy's percentage, 46%! (It's actually 46.01% to two decimal places.)

c) By now, you might suspect that the average speed is not just the average of the speeds! Average speed is the total number of miles shared out equally across the total number of hours. Because the journey at the slower speed takes more hours, it will have a greater weighting in finding the overall average speed. So, the overall average will be less than the mean of 50 mph and 30 mph, i.e. less than 40 mph. For example, assume the journey is 150 miles. The outward trip takes 3 hours, the return takes 5 hours. The total journey is 300 miles in 8 hours. The average speed is $300 \div 8 = 37.5$ mph. Again, imagine a silly example. Say the outward journey of 150 miles is done at 1500 mph and the return journey at 1 mph! The whole journey of 300 miles takes 150.1 hours, which gives an average speed of just under 2 mph. Clearly, the slower speed, with the greater journey time, has the greater weighting!

See also...

Check up 55: Weighted means

Summary of key ideas

◆ If a number of sets of numerical data are combined into a single set, the overall mean is the weighted mean of the component sets, with weightings equal to the number of items in each set.

◆ Similarly, if you know the percentages in various sets having a particular attribute, when you combine the sets the overall percentage is the weighted mean of the individual percentages, with weightings equal to the number of items in each set.

Further practice

56.1 (Use a calculator.) One spring term, the mean number of absences per day in a school were 5.6 for the 19 school days in January, 7.8 for the 20 school days in February, 8.1 for the 22 school days in March and 4.4 for the 5 days in April. What was the mean number of absences per day for the whole term?

56.2 The proportions of pupils present in a primary school one day are 78% in the Foundation Stage, 86% in Key Stage 1 and 94% in Key Stage 2. Do you need any further information to calculate the overall percentage of pupils present?

Check-Up

57

Understanding cumulative frequency graphs

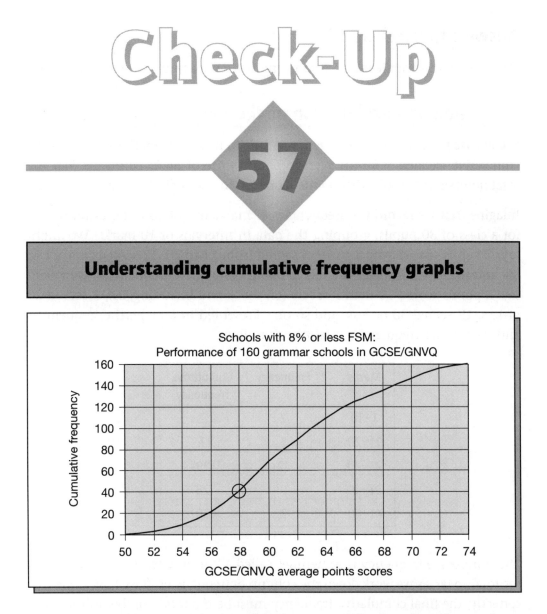

Schools with 8% or less FSM:
Performance of 160 grammar schools in GCSE/GNVQ

The diagram is a cumulative frequency graph showing data about the average points score achieved by 160 grammar schools in England in GCSE/GNVQ examinations one year. It passes through the point (58, 40), marked with a circle. What information does this point on the graph provide?

Answers to check-up 57

40 of the schools achieved an average points score of up to and including 58.

Discussion and explanation of check-up 57

Cumulative frequency is 'the frequency so far'. To read off from the graph that the cumulative frequency for an average points score of 56 is 20 means that the total number of schools with points scores up to and including that value is 20.

Imagine that we record the frequencies of marks out of 50 in an examination for a class of 30 pupils, grouping the data in intervals of 10 marks. We might say: 2 pupils scored from 1 to 10, 5 scored from 11 to 20, 12 scored from 21 to 30, and so on. If, however, we talked about cumulative frequencies, we would say: 2 pupils scored 10 marks or less (or, up to and including 10), 7 scored 20 or less, 19 scored 30 or less, and so on. Presented in a table, the frequencies and cumulative frequencies might be as follows:

Marks	Frequency	Cumulative frequency
1–10	2	2
11–20	5	7
21–30	12	19
31–40	9	28
41–50	2	30

The cumulative frequency is sometimes called a 'running-total'. We just add up the total so far, as we work down the column of frequencies. If we have done this correctly, the final cumulative frequency must be the total number in the set.

A cumulative frequency graph should always use the vertical axis to represent the cumulative frequency. The scale on this axis will go from zero to the total number in the set. The cumulative frequency graph given in this check-up has a shape that is very characteristic of such graphs. These are the kinds of statements we could make from this particular graph:

◆   About half the schools (80 schools) had an average points score of up to and including 61.

◆ About 146 of the schools were in the range 50 to 70 points; about 14 schools scored over 70.

Very often the cumulative frequencies will be expressed as percentages. So, instead of being labelled 0–160, the vertical axis in this check-up would be labelled 0–100%. See Further Practice.

See also...

Check-up 58: Cumulative frequency graphs, finding the median and quartiles

---

Summary of key ideas

◆ Cumulative frequency is a running total, that is, the total frequency so far.

◆ A cumulative frequency graph usually has the cumulative frequency on the vertical axis.

◆ The scale on this axis will go from zero to the total number in the set.

◆ Often this scale will be labelled in percentages, in which case it will be from 0% to 100%.

Further practice

57.1

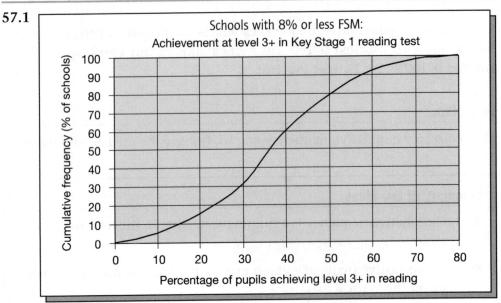

Schools with 8% or less FSM:
Achievement at level 3+ in Key Stage 1 reading test

Cumulative frequency (% of schools)

Percentage of pupils achieving level 3+ in reading

a) This cumulative frequency graph passes through the point (40, 60). Complete the following statements arising from this point on the graph:

'_____ % of schools with ___% or less of their pupils eligible for free school meals had up to and including ___% of their pupils achieving level 3+ in the Key Stage 1 reading test.'

b) About what percentage of these schools had more than 50% of their pupils achieving level 3+ in the reading test?

c) The Ford Primary School, with 7% FSM, had 45% of their pupils achieving level 3+ in reading. How did this compare with other schools in this group?

Check-Up

58

Cumulative frequency graphs, finding the median and quartiles

a) From the cumulative frequency graph given in Check-up 57, what were the lower quartile, median and upper quartile for the average points scores of the 160 grammar schools?

b) From the cumulative frequency graph given in Further Practice question 57.1, what were the lower quartile, median and upper quartile for the percentages of pupils achieving level 3 for reading in this group of schools? What were the 40th and 60th percentiles?

Answers to check-up 58

a) Median = 61 points, LQ = 58 points, UQ = 65.5 points, approximately.

b) Median = 36%, LQ = 26%, UQ = 47%, 40th %ile = 33%, 60th %ile = 40%, approximately.

Discussion and explanation of check-up 58

Cumulative frequency graphs are very convenient for reading off medians, quartiles and percentiles. The graph for Check-up 57 related to data from 160 schools. Reading from 80 (50% of the schools), 40 (25%) and 120 (75%) on the vertical axis to the corresponding values on the horizontal axis gives us the median, LQ and UQ for this data. For example, we read off that the bottom 40 schools (the bottom 25% of the population) achieved an average points score of up to and including 58. This is just another way of saying that the lower quartile was 58.

It is even easier when the cumulative frequencies are already given as percentages, as in Further Practice 57.1. Then we just read off the LQ as the value

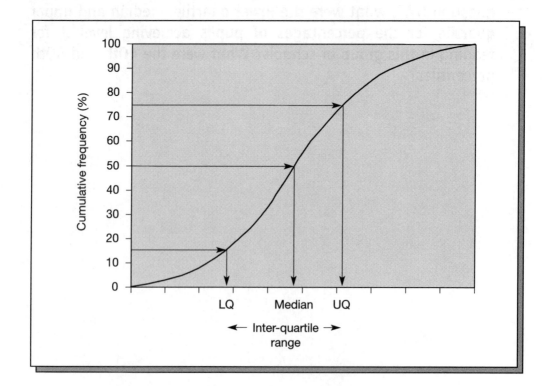

corresponding to a cumulative frequency of 25%, the median as the value corresponding to 50%, and the UQ as the value corresponding to 75%. This is summarized in the diagram above.

We can also read off any other percentiles directly from a cumulative frequency graph. In Further Practice 57.1, from 60% on the cumulative frequency axis we can read off the corresponding proportion of pupils as being 40%. This means that 60% of the schools had up to and including 40% of their pupils achieving level 3+ in reading. Put another way, we could say that the 60th percentile for these schools was 40% of their pupils achieving level 3+ for reading. This means, for example, that if my school achieved 41% at level 3+ for reading, then we exceeded the 60th percentile and we were therefore in the top 40% of schools, on the basis of this particular variable.

See also...

Check-up 44: Medians

Check-up 45: Upper and lower quartiles

Check-up 49: Percentiles

Summary of key ideas

◆   In a cumulative frequency graph, the lower quartile is the value on the horizontal axis corresponding to a cumulative frequency of 25% on the vertical axis, the median is the value corresponding to 50%, and the upper quartile is the value corresponding to 75%.

◆   Other percentiles can be read off directly as well; for example, from a cumulative frequency of 95% on the vertical axis the corresponding value on the horizontal axis is the 95th percentile.

Further practice

58.1 Complete the following summary of the data provided in the cumulative frequency graph below:

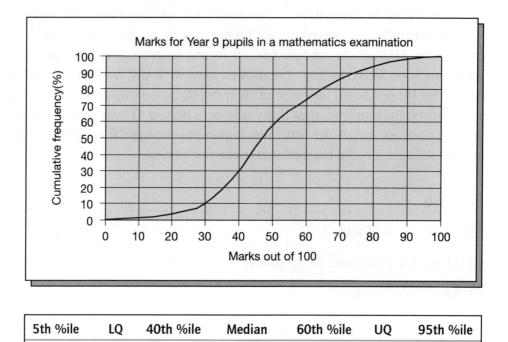

5th %ile	LQ	40th %ile	Median	60th %ile	UQ	95th %ile

How well, compared to the year group as a whole, did a pupil do who scored 82%?

Check-Up

59

The government has set targets of 75% of pupils achieving level 4+ for mathematics and 80% for English by the year 2002.

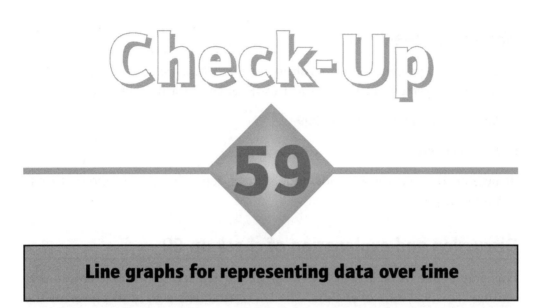

a) How far short of these targets were the national results in 1996? How far short were they in 2000?

b) In which year and in which subject was there the greatest rise from the previous year's results?

c) If the rate of progress indicated by these graphs continues over the next two years, does it seem likely that these targets will be achieved?

d) How do these graphs give a misleading impression of the rate of increase in the percentages of pupils achieving level 4+ in these subjects at Key Stage 2?

Answers to check-up 59

a) In 1996, 23 percentage points short for English, 21 short for mathematics. In 2000, 5 percentage points short for English, 3 for mathematics.

b) Mathematics from 1998 to 1999.

c) It looks likely.

d) Because the vertical axis does not start at zero, the graphs appear to rise more steeply.

Discussion and explanation of check-up 59

Line graphs like those in this check-up are particularly appropriate when presenting statistical data over time. The horizontal axis is used to represent the passing of time. Each item of data refers to a value of some variable (such as frequency in this example) recorded at a particular moment in time. In this case it is a year, but in other examples it could be a term, a month, a week, a day, and so on. The value of the variable is then represented by a point. Because the horizontal axis represents the passing of time, joining up these points with lines then gives an instant picture of how the variable changes with the passing of time. In this example, we can see immediately that over the years there have been gradual rises in the proportions of pupils reaching level 4+ in Key Stage 2 English and mathematics. We can also see at a glance the blip in the mathematics results in 1998, conveniently occurring just before the widespread implementation of the Numeracy Strategy and the consequent sharp rise in the results the following year.

The graphs enable us to recognise past *trends*, such as 'the proportion achieving level 4+ in English has been consistently higher than that for mathematics' and 'in general, there has been a steady increase in the percentages for both subjects over the last five years of results'. They may also be used (cautiously) to *extrapolate* for the future: 'if these trends continue we might expect to reach the targets of 80% for English and 75% for mathematics by the year 2002'.

If you look back at the bar charts shown in Check-ups 6, 7 and 8, you will notice that the frequencies on the vertical scale always start at zero. This is good practice. If you do not do this (a practice called *suppression of zero*), you produce a distorted picture of the relationships between the data. The same thing can happen with line graphs for representing frequencies over time. In the graphs used in this check-up, the zero on the vertical axis has been suppressed, by starting the scale at 50%. This gives a false impression of the rate of progress, making the lines appear much steeper than they would be if the scale started at 0%. (Try drawing these line-graphs yourself with the scale from 0% to see what I mean.) It would be cynical of me to suggest that any official body or newspaper would deliberately present statistics in a such a misleading way as this…

See also…

Check-up 6: Bar charts and frequency tables for discrete data

---

Summary of key ideas

◆ A line graph is an appropriate way for showing changes in a variable (such as frequency) over a period of time.

◆ The horizontal axis is used to represent the times (years, months, and so on) at which the values of the variable are recorded.

◆ A line graph can be used to identify past trends and to make cautious extrapolations for the future.

◆ Suppressing zero on the vertical axis, when this represents frequency, can be misleading.

Further practice

59.1

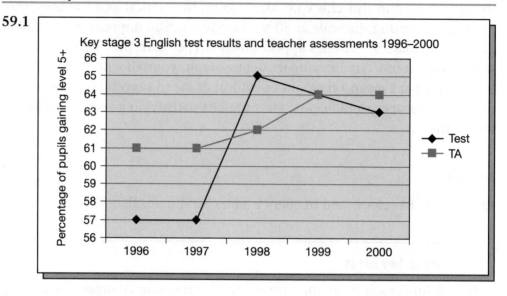

At the end of each of Key Stages 1, 2 and 3 pupils are assessed both by national tests and by teacher assessment. The graph shows the percentages of pupils assessed at level 5+ for English in the tests and in teacher assessments (TA) over five years.

a) What is the most obvious difference in the trends for test results and teacher assessments over these five years?

b) What happened in 1998 that might require some explanation?

c) What happened for the first time in 1999?

d) In what way are these graphs slightly misleading?

59.2 Which of these would appropriately be shown in a line graph:

a) the percentages of a school's timetabled time given over to various subjects

b) the numbers of pupils in a school with birthdays in particular months

c) the number of absences each week for a school over the 14 weeks of a term?

Check-Up

60

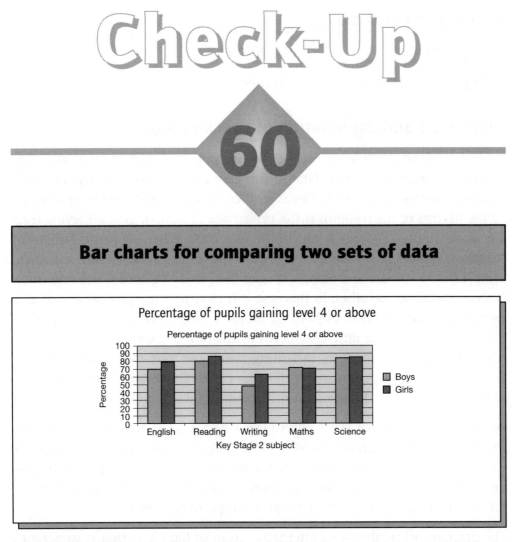

Percentage of pupils gaining level 4 or above

The graph shown compares the performances of boys and girls in terms of achievement at level 4 or above in the Key Stage 2 tests in the year 2000.

a) In which area was the proportion of boys reaching level 4+ higher than that of girls?

b) In which area was the disparity between the proportions of boys and girls the greatest?

c) What was the difference in percentage points between boys and girls in this area?

d) Approximately, what was the ratio of the percentages of boys to the percentage of girls achieving level 4+ in this area?

Answers to check-up 60

a) Only in maths.

b) Writing.

c) 15 percentage points.

d) About 3:4.

Discussion and explanation of check-up 60

As shown in the graph for this check-up, we can use bar charts to make comparisons between two sets of data. In this case we have data for boys and girls separately, for five areas of the Key Stage 2 curriculum. The variable represented by the heights of the columns is the percentage of boys or girls achieving level 4 or above in the Key Stage 2 tests in the year 2000. When we particularly want to make comparisons it makes sense to draw the columns side by side, as shown, using different colours or shadings. We can then see at a glance where one group is above or below the other. In this case it is clear that the proportions of girls exceed the proportions of boys in all subjects except mathematics. In mathematics and science the difference between the proportions of boys and girls is relatively small. The disparity in writing stands out very clearly. Only 48% of boys reached level 4+, compared with 63% of girls. The difference in the heights of the columns is the difference in percentage points, namely 15%.

Because the vertical axis starts at zero (see Check-up 59), we can also compare the heights of the columns by ratio. The height of the column for boys for writing looks to me to be only about three-quarters of the height of the column for girls. So, we could deduce from a quick glance at the graph that the ratio of the boys' proportion to the girls' proportion is about 3:4.

The diagram below shows an alternative form of bar chart that is sometimes used to represent two sets of data of this kind. This is not so useful for making quick comparisons between boys and girls. This kind of representation is probably more useful if what you are interested in mainly is how the boys and girls did separately in the various subjects. But in that case, you might as well just draw two separate bar charts!

You will also sometimes see bar charts for two sets of data drawn with 'stacked columns', as in Further Practice 60.1. This form of graph is used only when the purpose is first to show the overall totals in each category, and then, secondly, to compare the contributions of each of two or more components (e.g. values for boys and girls) to the total in each category.

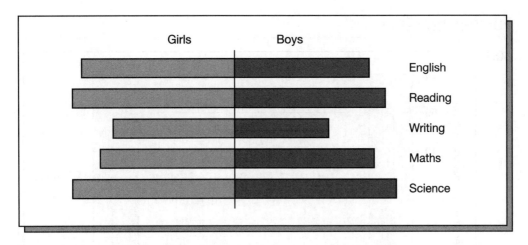

See also...

Check-ups 6–8: Bar charts...

Check-up 39: Increasing or decreasing by a percentage

Summary of key ideas

◆ A bar chart can be used to make comparisons between two sets of data (such as results in various subjects for boys and girls separately), by drawing columns side by side.

◆ Comparisons between the heights of columns might be made in terms of difference or (provided the vertical axis starts at zero) ratio.

◆ Stacked-column bar charts are used to show the contributions of two or more components to an overall total in each category.

Further practice

60.1

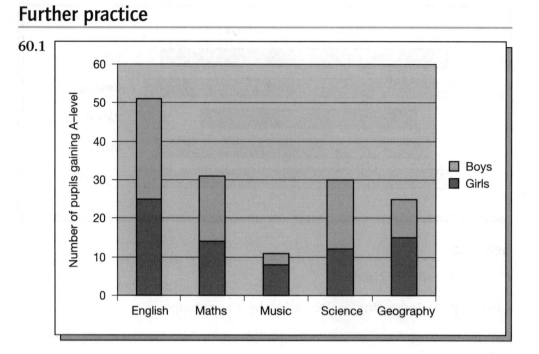

This graph displays the numbers of pupils in a sixth form gaining A-levels in various subjects, showing also how these numbers are split between boys and girls. What are the particular reasons for using a stacked-column graph here, rather than having the columns for girls and boys alongside each other?

The notion of value-added

The following table shows the points assigned by the DfES to various levels achieved in Key Stage 3 tests for English, mathematics and science:

Level	3 or below	3	4	5	6	7	8	Exceptional performance
Points	15 (21 for Eng)	21	27	33	39	45	51	57

The following table (all numbers rounded to the nearest whole number) shows the percentages of pupils in various groups, based on their 1998 Key Stage 3 average points score (APS), achieving various grades in GCSE English in the year 2000:

1998 KS3 APS	U	G	F	E	D	C	B	A	A*
25 or less	3	12	29	35	17	3	0	0	0
26–30	1	2	8	28	40	19	2	0	0
31–33	0	1	2	10	34	40	11	1	0
34–37	0	0	0	2	15	44	31	7	0
38 or more	0	0	0	0	2	16	40	32	9

Comment on the performance of a girl who achieved levels 7, 5, 4 for English, maths and science respectively in the 1998 Key Stage 3 tests and grade A in GCSE English in 2000.

Answers to check-up 61

She had an APS in 1998 of 35, putting her in the 34–37 APS group. In this group only 7% of pupils scored grade A or higher in English in 2000. So, compared to pupils with similar average points scores in 1998 she has done very well in English GCSE.

Discussion and explanation of check-up 61

The concept of 'value-added' is an uncomfortable metaphor for most teachers. It could be interpreted as treating pupils as a commodity whose value is judged by their level of attainment. On the other hand, it seems to treat education as a commodity, with the pupils as consumers and the value of education assessed only in terms of achievement in tests and examinations. The notion underpinning the whole concept is that it is possible to measure what 'value' a school has added to a pupil in a key stage by a number that indicates their progress through the levels of attainment, based on national tests. However, it is clear that it is much more likely that a pupil starting at, say, level 5, will improve by two levels during Key Stage 3, than it is that a pupil starting at level 2 will manage this. So, the simplistic idea of 'value-added' has had to be modified to take into account the range of performance that might be achieved by pupils in various groups based on their starting-points.

This check-up illustrates the kind of value-added data with which schools in England are provided annually by the DfES standards unit. First, a pupil is placed in a group based on their results in the previous key stage tests or examinations, using a points system such as the one shown. To take another example, a boy gaining levels 3, 5 and 5 for Key Stage 3 English, mathematics and science in 1998 would have an average points score of $(21 + 33 + 33)/3 = 29$. This puts him in the group with APS in the range 26–30. Now assume this boy gets grade E for English. From the next table, we can see that, of the pupils in this group, 28% gained grade E and 11% $(1 + 2 + 8)$ gained lower grades than this. The purpose of this data is to inform judgements about how well he has done in GCSE English compared to pupils starting from a similar base in terms of Key Stage 3 APS. The data shows that he is in the bottom 40%. So more than 60% of pupils in this group got a higher grade.

The examples of this boy and the girl quoted in the check-up show an obvious flaw in this process. English is clearly the girl's strongest subject; for the boy, it is his weakest. For pupils like this, with a spread of levels of attainment, the APS based on three subjects is unlikely to be a good predictor of their performance in individual subjects.

See also...

Check-up 54: Substituting into formulas

Check-up 62: Interpreting value-added graphs

Summary of key ideas

◆   Value-added data is intended to enable a pupil's achievement at the end of a key stage to be judged against the performances of pupils with similar average achievements at the end of the previous stage.

◆   In this process, achievement is measured by awarding points for various levels of attainment in national tests or grades in examinations.

Further practice

61.1 The table below shows the percentages of pupils with various Key Stage 1 average points scores (APS) in 1996 gaining various Key Stage 2 levels in the mathematics test four years later. B stands for 'working below the level of the test' and N for 'not reaching level 2'.

a) What is meant by '14<=APS<16' and 'APS>=18'? What levels in Key Stage 2 mathematics were achieved by most pupils with Key Stage 1 average points score in each of these two ranges?

b) A 7-year-old girl scored 13 points for reading, 9 points for writing and 17 points for mathematics in 1996. What was her Key Stage 1 average points score? At the age of 11 she gained level 5 for mathematics. How did she do in terms of the data provided in this table?

KS1 APS	B	N	2	3	4	5	6
APS<12	11	6	3	47	30	2	0
12<=APS<14	1	1	1	35	56	6	0
14<=APS<16	0	0	0	17	66	17	0
16<=APS<18	0	0	0	6	59	34	0
APS>=18	0	0	0	1	32	65	1

Check-Up

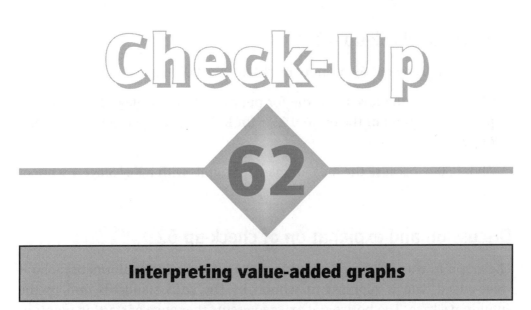

62

Interpreting value-added graphs

In the graph shown, the dotted lines represent upper and lower quartiles and the continuous line represents median values.

a) What can be said about the marks achieved in the Key Stage 2 English test in 2000 by the top 25% of pupils from the group who had a Key Stage 1 average points score of 15 in 1996?

b) Comment on a pupil with a Key Stage 1 average points score of 10 who achieved 30 marks in the Key Stage 2 English test.

c) Level 5 was awarded for a mark of 70+ in the Key Stage 2 English test. What proportion of pupils with a Key Stage 1 average points score of 17 achieved level 5?

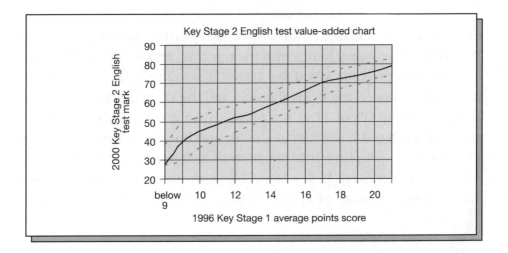

Answers to check-up 62

a) These pupils scored 69 or more marks in the 2000 English test.

b) This is below the lower quartile for pupils with a Key Stage 1 score of 10, putting this pupil in the bottom 25% for Key Stage 2 English for this group of pupils.

c) About 50%: because the median mark for pupils with a Key Stage 1 score of 17 is in fact 70.

Discussion and explanation of check-up 62

The graph in this check-up is typical of the way in which information about value-added data is supplied to schools by the DfES standards unit in the autumn package. The horizontal axis represents the range of starting points at the end of the previous key stage, in this case Key Stage 1, given in terms of the average points score (APS) in the national tests or tasks. In the case of the 1996 Key Stage 1 tests this would have been derived from levels achieved by pupils in reading, writing and mathematics. The vertical axis here represents the actual mark achieved in the 2000 Key Stage 2 English test. The bold line on the graph shows the median mark in this test for groups of pupils with various APSs in the Key Stage 1 tests four years earlier. This median mark clearly rises from about 27 up to about 79. When we get to an APS of 12 at Key Stage 1, for example, the median mark is about 52. What this means is that a pupil in this group scoring less than 52 marks came in the bottom 50% of this group in the Key Stage 2 English test, and a pupil scoring more than 52 marks came in the top 50%.

In a similar way, the dotted lines show the quartiles, allowing us to compare the marks of individual pupils with the top 25%, middle 50% and bottom 25% of pupils with the same APS at Key Stage 1. For example, for pupils with an APS of 12 at Key Stage 1, the UQ is about 58 and the LQ about 44. This means that a pupil with an APS of 12 at Key Stage 1 who gets more than 58 in the Key Stage 2 English test has achieved a mark that is in the top quarter of pupils in this group. The simplistic interpretation of such data would be, for pupils with APS of 12 at Key Stage 1: Key Stage 2 English mark greater than 58 → much value added; Key Stage 2 English mark less than 44 → little value added.

Level 5 was awarded for a mark of 70-plus in the Key Stage 2 English test. The grid line for 70 meets the UQ line at just over 15. So less than a quarter of pupils with APS of 15 at Key Stage 1 achieve level 5 in Key Stage 2 English. This 70 grid line then meets the median line at 17. So about 50% of pupils with APS of 17 at Key Stage 1 achieve level 5 in Key Stage 2 English. Finally the 70 grid line meets the LQ line just past 19. So less than 25% of pupils with APS of 19 at Key Stage 1 fail to gain level 5 in the Key Stage 2 English test.

See also...

Check-up 45: Upper and lower quartiles

Check-up 61: The notion of value-added

Summary of key ideas

◆   A value-added line graph may show, for example, the median and quartiles for an end-of-key-stage assessment for pupils with various average points scores at the end of the previous key stage.

◆   This enables the achievement of a particular pupil in the end-of-key-stage assessment to be related to those of the top 25%, middle 50% and bottom 25% of pupils with the same average points score at the end of the previous key stage.

Further practice

62.1 The graph shows the median and quartiles for the total GCSE/GNVQ points score in the year 2000 for pupils with various Key Stage 3 average points scores in 1998.

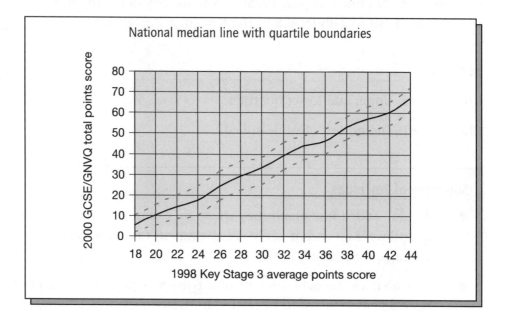

National median line with quartile boundaries

Give examples of total GCSE/GNVQ points scores that would put a pupil with a Key Stage 3 average points score of 40 (a) just in the top 25%, (b) clearly in the middle 50%, (c) just in the bottom 25%, for pupils who had the same Key Stage 3 score.

62.2 In terms of teachers making sensible professional judgements about the education and progress of individual pupils, most of the content of this and the previous check-up is:

A valuable and informative

B based on valid and reliable data about pupils' achievements

C meaningless nonsense.

Answers

Answers

Answers to further practice questions

1.1 $\frac{1}{10} = 10\%$ $\frac{3}{10} = 30\%$ $\frac{7}{10} = 70\%$ $\frac{9}{10} = 90\%$

$\frac{1}{5} = 20\%$ $\frac{2}{5} = 40\%$ $\frac{3}{5} = 60\%$ $\frac{4}{5} = 80\%$

$\frac{1}{8} = 12.5\%$ $\frac{3}{8} = 37.5\%$ $\frac{5}{8} = 62.5\%$ $\frac{7}{8} = 87.5\%$

$\frac{1}{20} = 5\%$ $\frac{3}{20} = 15\%$ $\frac{7}{20} = 35\%$ $\frac{9}{20} = 45\%$.

1.2 Multiplying by 4, '21 out of 25' is equivalent to '84 out of 100', or 84%. Multiplying by 5, '17 out of 20' is equivalent to '85 out of 100', or 85%. So, the second mark is the higher proportion of the total marks for the test.

1.3 For the first school, dividing by 6, '126 out of 600' is equivalent to '21 per hundred', or 21%. For the second school, '104 pupils out of 400' is '52 pupils per 200' or '26 pupils per 100', i.e. 26%. The second school has the larger proportion of pupils with English as an additional language.

2.1 For spelling, $\frac{19}{25} \rightarrow \frac{38}{50} \rightarrow \frac{76}{100} = 76\%$.

For mathematics, $\frac{42}{70} \rightarrow \frac{6}{10} \rightarrow 60\%$.

2.2 Unsatisfactory: $\frac{35}{250} \rightarrow \frac{7}{50} \rightarrow \frac{14}{100} = 14\%$.

Good: $\frac{130}{250} \rightarrow \frac{13}{25} \rightarrow \frac{26}{50} \rightarrow \frac{52}{100} = 52\%$.

Satisfactory: 100% − (14% + 52%) = 34%.

2.3   School R, 80%; School Q, 74%; School P, 60%.

3.1   The sequence should be 1.7, 1.8, 1.9, 2.0 (or 2), … the pupil is incorrectly thinking that after 'one point nine' comes 'one point ten'. The number 1.10 is the same as 1.1, which does not come after 1.9.

3.2   Tuesday and Wednesday have proportions greater than 0.08.

3.3   The target is less than 8%; Monday, 7.5%; Tuesday, 10%, Wednesday, 9%; Thursday, 7.9%; Friday, 0.9%.

4.1   a) The variable is the percentage of secondary schools whose attendance rates fall into various intervals.

b) The label 50–89% refers to those schools whose attendance rates were in the range 50–89%. The label 90–91% refers to schools whose attendance rates are in the range 90-91%, and so on. (Presumably these attendance rates have been expressed as percentages rounded to the nearest whole number.)

c) In Year 1, 17.6% of secondary schools had attendance rates in the range 92–93%.

d) 10.2% of secondary schools achieved attendance rates in the range 98-100% in Year 2. This was a higher proportion than in Year 1, where only 9.1% of secondary schools achieved attendance rates in this range.

e) It applied to 5.2% of secondary schools in Year 1 and 6.3% in Year 2.

5.1   a) 74, the total number of pupils who were absent for 5-9 days.

b) 3 were absent for 10 or more days, 34 (18 + 6 + 6 + 4) for less than 10 days.

c) 20 (15 + 4 + 1) were absent for 10 or more days, 245 (102 + 79 + 51 + 13) for less than 10 days.

d) No.

6.1   a) True.   b) False.   c) True.   d) False.   e) False.

7.1   a) This set of data could potentially contain a large number of different values, such as 5.0, 5.1, 5.2, 5.3, and so on; so it will probably have to be grouped into intervals, such as 5.0–5.2, 5.3–5.5, 5.6–5.8, and so on.

b) This variable will probably take only whole-number values from 0 to 10, so grouping will be unnecessary.

c) Point scores may take a large number of different values. An able pupil with nearly all A* and A grades in eight subjects might score around 60 points, for example. It will be necessary to group this data into intervals.

7.2 a) About 25   b) About 60   c) About 2000 classes.

d) No. The number of classes in this range is less than 1300, that is, less than 65% of the total.

8.1 b) and d) are continuous variables.

8.2 b) The stop-watch used to time the pupils will measure their times only to the nearest something. So, even though time-taken is theoretically a continuous variable, it might be rounded, for example, to the nearest tenth of a second. The times might range from about 14.5 up to maybe 24 seconds, so the rounded times could be grouped conveniently in intervals such as 14.5–15.4, 15.5–16.4, 16.5–17.4, and so on, giving about 10 groups for display in a bar chart. This is, of course, just one possible suggestion for handling the data.

d) A very rotund teacher might have, say, a girth of 110 cm and a height of 145 cm, giving a ratio of $\frac{110}{145}$ = 0.75862068966 on a calculator. By contrast, a super-model teacher might have a girth of only 50 cm but a height of 190 cm, giving a ratio of $\frac{50}{190}$ = 0.26315789474. It would be sufficient to round these ratios to two decimal places, suggesting a range of values from about 0.26 to 0.76. One way of grouping this rounded data then would be in intervals such as 0.25–0.29, 0.30–0.34, 0.35–0.39, and so on, giving possibly about 10 groups for display on a bar chart.

9.1 I would reply, 'Why don't you just count them?' However, if you are asked this daft question in a numeracy test the correct answer is 12.

9.2 32.

9.3 The calculator result is 113.74825, so the VAT payable is £113.75.

10.1 $\frac{1}{10}$ = 0.1 $\frac{3}{10}$ = 0.3 $\frac{7}{10}$ = 0.7 $\frac{9}{10}$ = 0.9

$\frac{1}{5}$ = 0.2 $\frac{2}{5}$ = 0.4 $\frac{3}{5}$ = 0.6 $\frac{4}{5}$ = 0.8

$\frac{1}{8}$ = 0.125 $\frac{3}{8}$ = 0.375 $\frac{5}{8}$ = 0.625 $\frac{7}{8}$ = 0.875

$\frac{1}{20}$ = 0.05 $\frac{3}{20}$ = 0.15 $\frac{7}{20}$ = 0.35 $\frac{9}{20}$ = 0.45.

10.2 a) $0.175 = \frac{175}{1000} = \frac{7}{40}$ $\qquad\qquad$ b) $0.007 = \frac{7}{1000}$.

10.3 Using a calculator, $\frac{4}{7} = 0.571$ (approximately), $\frac{879}{1500} = 0.586$. The second of these is the larger.

11.1 $5\% = \frac{1}{20}$ $\qquad$ $10\% = \frac{1}{10}$ $\qquad$ $18\% = \frac{9}{50}$ $\qquad$ $30\% = \frac{3}{10}$ $\qquad$ $37\% = \frac{37}{100}$.

11.2 $17.5\% = $ '17.5 in 100' = '35 in 200' $= \frac{35}{200} = \frac{7}{40}$ (cancelling 5). So VAT is applied at the rate of £7 in every £40.

11.3 12.5% is half of 25%, i.e. half of a quarter = one eighth $(\frac{1}{8})$. 87.5% must therefore be seven-eighths $(\frac{7}{8})$. The sum of the two fractions must be 1. It's worth memorizing these equivalents, as well as $\frac{3}{8} = 37.5\%$ and $\frac{5}{8} = 62.5\%$.

12.1 a) 48% of £75 gives the same result as 75% of £48, i.e. $\frac{3}{4}$ of £48 = £36.

b) 35% of £60 gives the same result as 60% of £35, i.e. $\frac{3}{5}$ of £35 = £21.

12.2 $895 \div 14.5$.

12.3 a) False: '28 sets of zero' gives zero, so $28 \times 0 = 0$.

b) True: note that $28 \times 0 = 0 \times 28$.

c) False: division by zero is meaningless.

d) True: $0 \div 28$ could mean 'how many sets of 28 pupils are needed to make zero pupils in total?' Answer: zero sets!

13.1 $30 - (18 - 10) = 30 - 8 = 22$, but $(30 - 18) - 10 = 12 - 10 = 2$.

Because these results are different, subtraction is not associative. In general, $A - (B - C)$ is not equal to $(A - B) - C$ (unless $C = 0$). The situation described corresponds to $30 - (18 - 10)$.

13.2 $160 \div (8 \div 4) = 160 \div 2 = 80$, but $(160 \div 8) \div 4 = 20 \div 4 = 5$.

Because these results are different, division is not associative. In general, $A \div (B \div C)$ is not equal to $(A \div B) \div C$ (unless $C = 1$ or -1).

13.3 $28 \times 25 = (7 \times 4) \times 25 = 7 \times (4 \times 25) = 7 \times 100 = 700$. Cost = £700.

14.1 (a) $(100 + 80) \times 8 = (100 \times 8) + (80 \times 8) = 800 + 640 = 1440$.

(b) $(200 - 20) \times 8 = (200 \times 8) - (20 \times 8) = 1600 - 160 = 1440$.

Cost = £1440.

14.2 a) First find the total cost of one each of the two books, £12 + £4 = £16, then multiply this by the number of pupils: 25 × £16 = £400.

b) First find the total cost of textbooks (25 × £12 = £300) and the total cost of workbooks (25 × £4 = £100), then add these: £300 + £100 = £400.

14.3 a) (£700 + £630) ÷ 7 = (£700 ÷ 7) + (£630 ÷ 7) = £100 + £90 = £190.

b) (£1400 – £70) ÷ 7 = (£1400 ÷ 7) – (£70 ÷ 7) = £200 – £10 = £190.

15.1 a) Doing the operations in the order entered, the four-function calculator would give the result as 3.

b) Giving precedence to the division, the scientific calculator would give the result as 9.

15.2 The operations have been done in the order entered. This is using a basic four-function calculator. The result displayed is correct in this context.

16.1 My estimate was around £84 (£20 + £9 + £15 + £36 + £4).

Actual cost = £85.75.

16.2 C looks most likely. We need less than £2 for each of less than 70 pupils, so the cost should be under £140. Actual cost is £131.92.

16.3 The calculator result of 181.7 has been misinterpreted as £181.07. It should be £181.70.

17.1 Calculator sequence: MRC, MRC, 4.15 × 5 =, M+, 2.95 × 3 =, M+, 5.45 × 3 =, M+, 3 × 12 =, M+, 0.95 × 4 =, M+, MRC.

17.2 10.

17.3 £554 869.

18.1 $\frac{38}{190} = \frac{2}{10} = 20\%$ (no calculator required)

$\frac{23}{190} = 0.12105263158 = 12.1\%$ to one decimal place

$\frac{19}{190} = \frac{1}{10} = 10\%$ (no calculator required)

$\frac{5}{190} = 0.02631578947 = 2.6\%$ to one decimal place

$\frac{1}{190} = 0.00526315789 = 0.5\%$ to one decimal place.

19.1 Females: C, 19.5%; D, 18.3%, E, 14.2%; N, 8.2%.
Males: C, 18.5%, D, 17.9%, E. 14.0%; N, 8.5%.

19.2   Giving these to the nearest whole percent would not discriminate suffi-ciently between the data. For example, both females and males would have 18% for grade D. It would also exaggerate some differences, e.g. giv-ing one whole percent difference between females and males in the N-grade category (using 8% and 9% respectively, instead of 8.2% and 8.5%).

20.1   To order these populations, look first at the power of 10 and then at the digits. The order is: UK, Japan, India, China.

20.2   £290 000 000 or £2.9 $\times$ 10^8.

20.3 $4.4820717 \times 10^{-3} = 0.0044820717$ = approximately 0.4%.

21.1   One method is to round the £4.95 up to £5. Then 24 $\times$ £5 = £120. Subtract 24 $\times$ 5p = £1.20. Answer £118.80.

21.2   One method is to use factors, writing 48 as 4 $\times$ 12. Then 125 $\times$ 4 = 500 and 500 x 12 = 6000. Answer £6000.

21.3   The 97 is close to 100, so think of it as 100 – 2 – 1. Then we need (240 $\times$ 100) – (240 $\times$ 2) – (240 $\times$ 1) = 24 000 – 480 – 240 = 23 520 – 240 = 23 280.

21.4 $45 \times 74 = 45 \times 2 \times 37 = 90 \times 37 = 100 \times 37 - 10 \times 37 = 3700 - 370 = 3330$
Area = 3330 square metres.

$44 \times 75 = 11$ x $2 \times 2 \times 75 = 11 \times 2 \times 150 = 11 \times 300 = 3300$
Area = 3300 square metres, which is smaller.

22.1   You could start by dividing both numbers by 3 to give 48 ÷ 3 = 16. Or you could think of the 144 as 180 – 36, which when divided by 9 gives 20 – 4 = 16. Or you could break the 144 up into 90 + 54, giving 10 + 6 = 16.

22.2   6035 ÷ 85 = 12070 ÷ 170 (doubling both numbers) = 1207 ÷ 17 (dividing by 10). To divide 1207 by 17, I would start with 1700 (100 $\times$ 17), which is 493 too much. The 493 can be split up into 340 + 153 = 340 + 170 – 17, each bit of which can be divided easily by 17. Answer: 100 – (20 + 10 – 1) = 71, i.e. £71 per pupil.

22.3   For 893 ÷ 24, I would start with 30 $\times$ 24 = 720. So I need another 173. Next, 5 $\times$ 24 = 120, so I need another 53. Then, 2 x 24 = 48, which leaves me just 5 short. The result is 30 + 5 + 2 = 37, with 5 remainder. This 5 is less than half a mark per pupil, so to the nearest whole number the aver-age mark is 37.

23.1 a) 12.5% of 160 = $\frac{1}{8}$ of 160 = 20; b) 30% of 220 = $\frac{3}{10}$ of 220 = 66.

23.2 50% = 120; 25% = 60; 1% = 2.4; 2% = 4.8. Adding these, 78% = 187.2. So about 187 pupils, or 188 to pass the target.

23.3 The percentage not reaching level 4 is 100% – 40% – 36% = 24%. So we need 24% of 125. 20% = $\frac{1}{5}$ which is 25; 4% = $\frac{1}{25}$ which is 5. Total = 30.

24.1 Key sequence for first method: $279 \times 47.8 \div 100 =$
Key sequence for second method: 279×47.8 % (procedure not universal)
Key sequence for third method: $0.478 \times 279 =$
The result is 133.362, so to surpass this percentage 134 pupils must achieve the required grades.

25.1 Stepping from 14.87 to 14.9 to 15 to 20 and then to 100, the difference between 14.87% and 100% is 0.03 + 0.1 + 5 + 80 = 85.13%.

25.2 2.970 + 34.000 + 1.085 = 38.055 m.

25.3 3.620 – 2.085 = 1.535 m.

26.1 132.

26.2 330.

27.1 The areas method gives four multiplications: 20×30, 20×9, 8×30, 8×9, giving 600 + 180 + 240 + 72 = 1092 hours.

27.2 The areas method gives six multiplications: 100×70, 100×2, 40×70, 40×2, 2×70, 2×2, giving 7000 + 200 + 2800 + 80 + 140 + 4 = 10 224 square metres, just larger than a hectare.

28.1 I subtracted first 10 classes of 28 (280), leaving 364, then another 10, leaving 84, then 2 classes of 28 (56), leaving 28, which was 1 more class. In total this gave 10 + 10 + 2 + 1 = 23 classes.

28.2 I subtracted first 20 coach-loads of 42 (840), leaving 710, then another 10 (420), leaving 290, then 5 coach-loads of 42 (210), leaving 80, which was 1 more coach-load with 38 remainder. In total this gave 20 + 10 + 5 + 1 = 36 coach-loads, with 38 remainder. So, 37 coaches are needed.

29.1 $1 \times 2 \times 3 \times 4 \times 5 = 120 \rightarrow 0.1 \times 0.2 \times 0.3 \times 0.4 \times 0.5 = 0.00120$ (with five figures after the point). This can be written as 0.0012, but don't drop the final zero until *after* you have decided where to put the point.

29.2 $0.6 \times 0.12 \rightarrow 6 \times 12 = 72 \rightarrow 0.072$.

29.3 12% on FSM, 60% of these, no adult in employment.
60% of 12% = 7.2% (50% of 12 is 6, 10% of 12 is 1.2, add these to get 60% of 12).

29.4 $0.71 \times 0.71 = 0.5041$, so the area of the paper is reduced by a factor of about 0.5. This is consistent with the fact that a sheet of A5 paper is half of a sheet of A4.

30.1 $0.126 \div 0.09 = 126 \div 90 = 14 \div 10 = 1.4$ or 140%.

30.2 a) is the same (both numbers doubled), c) is the same (both multiplied by 100), and d) is the same (both divided by 10).

30.3 a) 2   b) 0.2   c) 200   d) 0.002.

31.1 B: the actual cost is £315.21.
Calculators will cost about £120, transparencies about £24, envelopes about £8, which is £152 in total. VAT is less than a fifth of this, say, a bit less than £30, making about £180 in total. Add about £135 for the dictionaries (I used $15 \times £9$), giving about £315 in total.

31.2 To the nearest percent: 93%, 57%, 33%, 34%, 12%. Estimates within 2% either side of these are very good.

32.1 One possibility is 08.55–09.05 registration, 09.05–09.25 mental arithmetic, 09.30–10.20 mathematics, 10.45–11.00 free time, 11.00–11.55 English.

32.2 Taught-week = 22.5 hours, 1 hour short of the recommended 23.5 hours.

33.1 1189 mm = 118.9 cm = 1.189 m.

33.2 a) about 17.5 cm, b) about 20 m, c) about 20 mm.

33.3 70 mph is just over 110 kilometres per hour, so a journey of about 10 000 km will take around 90 hours. Since you also travel through 90° of latitude on this journey, this means that when you are travelling due south (or north) at 70 mph you are moving through about 1° of latitude per hour.

34.1 A5 paper is approximately 149 mm by 210 mm, or 0.149 m by 0.210 m. These dimensions give the area as approximately $0.149 \times 0.21 = 0.03129$ m^2. The fraction $\frac{1}{32}$ as a decimal is 0.03125.

34.2   The volume is $0.175 \times 0.095 \times 0.065 = 0.0010806$ m^3, which is just over 0.001 m^3, or one thousandth of a cubic metre, or 1000 cm^3. (NB: 1 litre $= 1000$ cm^3.)

34.3   1 ha = about $2\frac{1}{2}$ acres. 0.4 ha = 4000 m^2, which could be 40 m $\times$ 100 m, or 80 m $\times$ 50 m, 160 m $\times$ 25 m, and so on.

35.1   £6.50 for half a litre is £13 per litre. £5 for 400 ml is £1.25 for 100 ml, so £12.50 for 1 litre. On this basis, the second is the better buy.

35.2   1.25 dl = 0.125 litres = 125 ml = 25 medicine-spoonfuls.

35.3   a) a quarter of a pound, b) 330 ml, c) 40 litres, d) 70 kg (which is about 11 stone).

35.4   An A4 sheet is $\frac{1}{16}$ of a square metre in area (half of A3, which is half of A2, which is half of A1, which is half of A0, which is 1m^2 in area). So its weight is $\frac{1}{16}$ of 80 g = 5g. A ream is 500 sheets, so weighs 2500 g = 2.5 kg. You can safely put 8 sheets of standard A4 paper (40 g) in an envelope (less than 20 g) and stay within the 60-g limit. This is a useful piece of knowledge!

36.1   50 Swiss francs per pupil is 2100 Swiss francs in total.

36.2   The teacher can buy 14 marker pens, costing £17.50 in total. My mental starting point was 4 for £5.

36.3   The total cost is £556.80, which is £560 to the nearest £10. I assumed that I would not be far out if I let the lapel badge cost 25p. That's £1.75 per pupil, £3.50 for 2, £7 for 4. Multiply this by 80, to get £560 for 320 pupils. This is obviously £3.20 over the actual cost.

36.4   The teacher has enough in the budget to buy 31 textbooks. I started this mental calculation by thinking that 30 at £13 would be £390. So, 30 at £12.90 would be £3 less than this, i.e. £387. That leaves £13, enough to buy one more textbook.

37.1   The difference is £24,500. The ratio is 42 000:17 500, which could be simplified in various ways, such as 420:175 = 84:35 = 12:5 = 24:10. This is 2.40:1, or £2.40 for every £1.

37.2   The difference is now £25,382. But the ratio is still 2.40:1. Notice that applying a percentage-increase increases the difference, but leaves the ratio the same. Those on higher salaries would prefer this kind of pay rise.

37.3   The difference is still £25,382. But the ratio is now 2.36:1. Notice that applying a flat-rate increase of this kind leaves the difference the same, but reduces the ratio. Those on lower salaries would prefer this kind of pay rise.

38.1   The £4800 must be divided by 8 (1 + 2 + 5), giving £600. The allocations are £600, £1200 and £3000 for nursery, infant and junior respectively.

38.2   Girls: $\frac{4}{7}$ = 57.1% approximately. Boys: $\frac{3}{7}$ = 42.9% approximately. Number of girls = 41 000 ÷ 7 × 4 = about 23 400. Number of boys = 41 000 ÷ 7 × 3 = about 17 600.

39.1   61%, 58.8%.

39.2   6543 × 1.21 and 6543 × 0.79.

39.3   It makes no difference! The price in both cases is £815.83.
VAT first is: 789 × 1.175 × 0.88. Reduction first is: 789 × 0.88 × 1.175.

40.1   The increase is £150, which is 12% of £1250.
After decreasing £1400 by 12% we should expect the answer to be less than £1250, because the reduction is 12% of £1400, whereas the previous increase was 12% of only £1250.
Calculator result: £1400 × 0.88 = £1232, which, as predicted, is less than £1250.

40.2   Science increases by 0.2; 0.2 ÷ 31.6 = 0.006 (approximately) = 0.6%.
Mathematics decreases by 1.8; 1.8 ÷ 32.9 = 0.055 (approximately) = 5.5%.

40.3   The proportion increases by 5 percentage points (54.4 – 49.4). Expressed as a percentage of the starting value, 5 ÷ 49.4 = 0.101 (approximately) = a 10.1% increase over the five years.
The biggest annual percentage increase was 3.7% from 1998 to 1999.

41.1   Note that the increase is not 26 *percentage points*, but 26% of the previous proportion. So 126% (of the previous proportion) = 63 (i.e. 63% of the pupils), which gives 2% = 1, so 100% = 50. So the previous proportion was 50%.

41.2   85.8% = 37 900, so 1% = 37 900 ÷ 85.8, and 100% = 37 900 ÷ 85.8 × 100. This gives 44 172.494, which is 44 200 to the nearest hundred.

42.1   The mean class-size for School X is 28.6; the mean class-size for School Y is 27.1. These might be calculated to compare the schools with some national data about mean class-sizes. Or, to see whether, on the whole, the schools are achieving some target for reduction of class-size; but the mean of 28.6 for School X will be little consolation for the teacher with a class of 35! All other things being equal (which is highly unlikely), a comparison might be made between the mean class-sizes of the schools as part of an evaluation of the impact of class-size on pupil achievement.

42.2 The total number of pupils is 129. To find the total number of points, note that there are sixteen 21s, thirty-two 27s, and so on. So, the total is found by calculating $(16 \times 21) + (32 \times 27) + (40 \times 33) + (25 \times 39) + (8 \times 45) + (6 \times 51) + (2 \times 57) = 4275$. So the mean is $4275 \div 129 = 33.1$ to one decimal place. Given all the other variables involved, this is a fairly meaningless statistic. It assumes, for example, that a school should get the same credit for two pupils gaining levels 4 and 8 respectively as for two pupils both gaining level 6. There is no valid basis for such an assumption.

43.1 The mode is level 4.

43.2 The mode was level 5.

43.3 The modal interval is £4.00–£5.99.

44.1 This school is in the 'FSM more than 50%' group. Compared to schools in this group, the results in terms of A*–C grades for GCSE mathematics are 'better than average', because their 28% is higher than the median of 18%; i.e. this school did better than at least half of the schools in this group.

44.2 St Anne's devotes 22.1% of the Y3 teaching week to English. This is less than the median percentage for all primary schools. More than half of all schools devote a larger percentage of the Y3 teaching week to English than does St Anne's.

45.1 Compared to schools in this FSM group, with 28% achieving grade C or above in mathematics, the first school has a proportion higher than the UQ (25%). With 15% achieving this level, the second school has a proportion lying between the LQ (12%) and the median (18%). Loosely speaking, the first school has done well compared to similar schools, being in the top quarter based on the proportions of pupils gaining grade C or above in mathematics. The second school is only 'fairly average', below the median but not in the bottom quarter of these schools.

45.2 The percentage of the Y3 teaching week for English at St Anne's (22.1%) is just less than the LQ (22.2%) for all primary schools. This puts them in the bottom quarter of schools in terms of the proportion of the Y3 teaching week devoted to English. The proportion for St Michael's (30%) exceeds the UQ (28.1%) for all primary schools, putting them in the top quarter for this variable. Loosely speaking, St Anne's has a low proportion of the Y3 week devoted to English, whereas St Michael's has a high proportion.

46.1 The 'average' numbers of hours for RE and PE given by the median values are very similar. However, there is much more variation between schools in the time given to PE than there is in the time given to RE. The range for PE (1.7 hours) is greater than that for RE (1.3 hours). Also, the IQR for PE (0.7 hours) is greater than that for RE (0.4 hours), suggesting that the greater variability is not just due to a few schools giving an exceptionally high number of hours to PE.

47.1 A is valid. The maximum marks achieved were 91 and 100 for literacy and numeracy respectively.

B is invalid. The median marks were about 40 and 60 for literacy and numeracy respectively.

C is invalid. The diagram does not tell us anything about how individual pupils did in the tests.

D is invalid. A mark of 40 in literacy was bettered by about 75% of the pupils, whereas 40 in numeracy was the median mark.

E is valid. A mark of 70 in literacy is in the 'fairly average' box, whereas a mark of 70 in numeracy is in the 'high-scoring' whisker.

F is probably valid. The numeracy box (the middle 50% of pupils) and the bottom whisker (the bottom 25%) are substantially lower than the literacy box and lower whisker.

G is invalid. It should be the lowest 50 scores, i.e. the bottom 25%.

H is valid. The top whisker for numeracy is much longer than that for literacy.

48.1 a) The bottom plot refers to 'all schools in England with Y6 pupils with 8% or less pupils eligible for FSM' and the top plot refers to 'all schools in England with Y6 pupils with more than 50% of pupils eligible for FSM'. The variable in both cases is the percentage of pupils achieving level 4 or above in the Key Stage 2 English national assessment that year.

b) Based on the percentages of pupils achieving level 4 or above in Key Stage 2 English, the top 25% of schools in the group with 8% or less FSM had proportions of pupils achieving this level ranging from about 93% to 100%. Based on the percentages of pupils achieving level 4 or above in Key Stage 2 English, the middle 50% of schools in the group with more than 50% FSM had proportions of pupils achieving this level ranging from about 46% to 67%.

c) There is a very striking contrast between the performances of the two groups. The boxes (the middle 50%) do not even overlap. All the schools in the first group scored higher in terms of the variable than the median for the second group. To put this another way, more than half the schools in the second group had a lower proportion of pupils achieving this level for English than the lowest proportion achieved by any school in the first group (60%). And the highest proportion achieved by any school in the second group (87%) was equal to the median for the first group and was therefore equalled or surpassed by at least half of the schools in that group.

d) Hay is in the bottom 25% of schools in their FSM group and has therefore done poorly in English compared with similar schools. Lock is in the top 25% of schools in their FSM group and has therefore done well in English compared with similar schools.

49.1 a) The top 40% of schools, based on their Key Stage 1 results for reading, had average points scores of 16.2 or more; the bottom 60% had average points scores of 16.2 or less.

b) Clarendon Primary was in the top 40% based on average points scores for Key Stage 1 reading, but not in the top 25%. But for writing they were in the top 5%.

c) At least 5% of the schools, which is about 800 schools or more.

49.2 If all the non-selective secondary schools in this FSM group were ranked according to the proportions of pupils gaining grade C or above in GCSE science, then a school coming nine-tenths of the way along the line would have about 69% of their pupils gaining these grades in science. In other words, the top tenth of schools would have 69% or more of their pupils gaining these grades in science.

50.1 a) 5   b) 10   c) 2   d) 28.

e) 52% for boys and 72% for girls (this was actually for Art and Design) – a difference of 20 percentage points.

51.1 The points are generally clustered around a rising diagonal line, indicating a positive correlation. In regions C, E and G there are 4, 6 and 2 points, giving 12 out of 20 points in total; there are no points in regions A and J. This confirms a positive correlation.

51.2 a) A positive correlation might be expected. Older pupils would tend to be taller.

b) No correlation would be expected. I know of no reason why the size of the head should be related to the score in a numeracy test.

c) A negative correlation might be expected. The pupils living nearest would tend to leave home later; those living further away would tend to leave home earlier.

52.1 £87.50.

52.2 a) This is not direct proportion: a letter of 40 g will not cost twice as much as one of 20g, for example.

b) This is not direct proportion. A square of side 5 m has an area of 25 m^2; a square of side 10 m has an area of 100 m^2; the ratios 5:25 and 10:100 are not equal.

c) This is direct proportion. Weights in pounds to weights in kg are always in the same ratio, about 1:0.454.

d) This is not direct proportion, although it is sometimes difficult making parents understand this. A pupil at level 2 in Year 2 is unlikely to be at level 4 in Year 4, level 6 in Year 6 and level 8 in Year 8!

52.3 (0,0), (254,100), (127,50)…

The ratio is about 1:0.39 (using a calculator), so the gradient will be about 0.39. This means that 1 cm is about 0.39 of an inch.

53.1 Only (b) might be sensible, but this is assuming that each pupil can be located in one and only one ethnic origin group and that there are not too many different groups.

A pie chart could not be used for (a) because there is not a single population to be represented by the pie. A pie chart would be hopeless for (c) because there are 52 subsets!

53.2 a) third   b) half   c) walking.
d) bus (because 48 pupils = 20%).

54.1 a) About 61.
b) About 28.

The transposition of the digits here make these two results easy to remember as reference points for converting temperatures.

In (a) the 9C/5 must be calculated before adding on 32.

In (b) the (F – 32) bracket must be done first, before multiplying by 5 and dividing by 9.

55.1 a) $L = (2A + 5B + 2C + D)/10$.
b) $(2 \times 3 + 5 \times 4 + 2 \times 3 + 3)/10 = 35 \div 10 = 3.5$, which rounds up to level 4.
c) $(2 \times 5 + 5 \times 4 + 2 \times 5 + 4)/10 = 44 \div 10 = 4.4$, which also rounds to level 4.

Try explaining that to the parents! This is the kind of daft thing that happens when you reduce educational performance to a set of numbers.

56.1 $(5.6 \times 19 + 7.8 \times 20 + 8.1 \times 22 + 4.4 \times 5)/(19 + 20 + 22 + 5) = 7.01$.

56.2 You need to know how many pupils are in each of the three stages. Then find the weighted mean of the three percentages, using these numbers as weightings.

57.1 a) '60% of schools with 8% or less of their pupils eligible for free school meals had up to and including 40% of their pupils achieving level 3+ in the Key Stage 1 reading test.'
b) About 21% (100% – 79%).
c) The Ford School's percentage of pupils gaining level 3+ for reading equalled or bettered that of about 70% of schools in this FSM group.

This example of a cumulative frequency graph (not untypical of government statistics) is difficult to read, because it contains percentages used in three different ways: the percentage of pupils eligible for free schools meals (FSM), the percentage of pupils gaining level 3+ in reading, and the percentages of schools with various proportions of pupils achieving this level.

58.1 The numbers below are approximate:

5th %ile	LQ	40th %ile	Median	60th %ile	UQ	95th %ile
25	38	44	47	51	62	80

A score of 82% is above the 95th percentile, i.e. in the top 5% for the year group.

59.1 a) Teacher assessments have been fairly consistent, while test results have fluctuated markedly by comparison.

b) While the proportion achieving level 5+ by TA did not change much, there was a dramatic rise in the proportions reaching this level in the test. Explanations: teachers got better at preparing pupils for the test? The test got easier?

c) The proportions assessed at level 5+ by TA and by the test coincided.

d) By not starting at zero on the vertical axis a misleading impression can be given of the rate of change from one year to the next.

59.2 Only (c) is a variable changing with the passing of time, which would appropriately be represented in a line graph.

60.1 The first purpose of the graph is to compare the total numbers of pupils per A-level subject, shown by the heights of the columns. The second purpose is to show the contributions of boys and girls to these totals. For example, music is clearly the lowest frequency of these five subjects, but within this the contribution of the girls can be seen to be far greater than that of the boys.

61.1 a) '14 is less than or equal to the Key Stage 1 average points score, which is less than 16': this means an APS from 14 up to but not including 16. Most pupils in this group (66%) achieved level 4 in Key Stage 2 maths.

'Key Stage 1 average points score greater than or equal to 18'. Most pupils in this group (65%) achieved level 5 in Key Stage 2 maths.

b) Key Stage 1 APS = 13. Only 6% of pupils in this group achieved level 5 or above in Key Stage 2 maths.

62.1 a) 64

　　　b) Any score from 52 to 62; 57 is bang in the middle. c) 50

62.2 C, of course!

Sources of Data

Below is a list of the published sources of the data used in the check-ups and further practice questions in this book.

The Department for Education and Employment Autumn Packages for Schools, 1998, 1999, 2000, available at the DfES website: *www.standards.gov.uk/performance*

Check-ups 04, 11, 24b, 25a, 31b, 37c, 38c, 40c, 44, 45, 47, 48, 49, 54, 57, 58, 59, 61, 62

Further Practice 11.1, 31.2, 38.2, 40.3, 42.2, 44.1, 44.2, 45.1, 45.2, 48.1, 49.1, 49.1, 50.1, 57.1, 59.1, 61.1, 62.1

Other sections of the DfES website:

www.standards.gov.uk/genderandachievement

Check-up 60

www.standards.gov.uk/schoolimprovement

Further Practice 20.2

Qualifications and Curriculum Authority (1999) *Standards at Key Stage 2, English, Mathematics and Science, report on the 1998 National Curriculum assessments for 11-year-olds.* Sudbury: QCA Publications

Further Practice 20.3

Qualifications and Curriculum Authority (1999) *Standards at Key Stage 3, Mathematics, report on the 1998 National Curriculum assessments for 14-year-olds.* Sudbury: QCA Publications

Check-up 21

Further Practice 22.1

Qualifications and Curriculum Authority (2000) *Standards at Key Stage 2, English, Mathematics and Science, report on the 1999 National Curriculum assessments for 11-year-olds*. Sudbury: QCA Publications

Check-ups 20b, 24a

Further Practice 25.1

Qualifications and Curriculum Authority (2001) *Assessment and Reporting Arrangements Key Stage 2*. Sudbury: QCA Publications

Further Practice 55.1

School Curriculum and Assessment Authority (1996) *GCSE Results Analysis*. London: SCAA Publications

Check-up 19

School Curriculum and Assessment Authority (1996) *GCSE Results Analysis*. London: SCAA Publications

Check-up 30a